KATHERINE DUNHAM

KATHERINE DUNHAM

James Haskins

COWARD, MC CANN & GEOGHEGAN, INC.
NEW YORK

Copyright © 1982 by James Haskins
All rights reserved. This book, or parts thereof, may not be reproduced in any form without permission in writing from the publishers. Published simultaneously in Canada by General Publishing Co. Limited, Toronto. First printing. Printed in the United States of America
Designed by Nanette Stevenson

Library of Congress Cataloging in Publication Data
Haskins, James,
  Katherine Dunham.
  Includes index.
  Summary: Relates the life story of the famous choreographer who, wherever she has lived, has worked at bringing creative arts participation to the community.
  1. Dunham, Katherine—Juvenile literature.
2. Dancers—United States—Biography—Juvenile literature.
3. Choreographers—United States—Biography—Juvenile literature. [1. Dunham, Katherine. 2. Dancers.
3. Choreographers. 4. Afro-Americans—Biography] I. Title.
GV1785.D82H38 1981 793.3′2′0924 [B] [92] 81-15178
ISBN 0-698-20549-9 AACR2

Acknowledgments

*I am grateful to Pat McKissack, Jeanelle Stovall
and especially Kathy Benson for their help.
And of course this book would not have been possible
without the commitment and contributions of
John Pratt and Miss Katherine Dunham*

KATHERINE DUNHAM

 ONE

IN JULY 1967, KATHERINE DUNHAM AND MEMBERS OF A YOUTH gang called the Imperial War Lords met in a tavern in East St. Louis, Illinois. Afterward, as the youth who had arranged the meeting was walking her back to her car, two policemen arrived to arrest the young man, who was suspected of having smashed windows the night before. Katherine Dunham went to the police station with her young friend, insisting that his rights be observed. There was a scuffle, and Katherine was jailed on charges of disorderly conduct.

She was 58 years old at the time, but that is not what caused the incident to make headlines in newspapers across the nation. What caused newspaper editors to sit up and take notice when this story came over the wire services was that this was *the* Katherine Dunham, world-renowned dancer, choreographer, and anthropologist.

What was Katherine Dunham doing in a bar with a bunch of young street toughs? She was trying to get them off the street and into a program that would direct their energies away from crime and destructiveness and into self-discipline and self-pride. Amidst the graffiti-marked walls and vacant lots of a city slum that was beyond the imagination of the most destitute resident of Watts or Newark, Katherine Dunham was building a Performing Arts Training Center for the people of East St. Louis.

Fifteen years later, she is still at it. Although there is still graffiti on the walls of East St. Louis, boards on the burned-out buildings, too much crime, too many gangs, and too few jobs, there exists a fifteen-year-old Performing Arts Training Center as well as a five-year-old Katherine Dunham Museum, and the lives of hundreds of East St. Louisians, young and old, have been changed by Katherine Dunham.

In earlier years, Katherine Dunham changed other people's lives in other ways. She brought to people all over the world the experience of the black cultural heritage; she brought to dancers and lovers of dance an awareness that dance isn't just ballet but the expression in movement of the traditions and cultures of peoples. She trained two generations of black dancers and paved the way for modern black dance companies, not to mention dance companies of other ethnic groups. She is considered to have influenced dancing on Broadway and in Hollywood and to be responsible for the distinctly American quality of American dance. But she feels her greatest work of all has been done in East St. Louis, Illinois, with kids whose previous idea of dance was boogeying. Katherine Dunham is a remarkable woman indeed.

How did she get to East St. Louis? The same way she got from the slums of Chicago to Northwestern University, from the bush country of Haiti to dance stages around the world, from Hollywood to the Metropolitan Opera. But you have to read it to believe it. Here is the story of Katherine Dunham.

TWO

KATHERINE DUNHAM KNEW ABOUT POVERTY AND DESPAIR AT an early age. But she also knew that music and singing and dancing could take the edge off the sad things in life. Both her mother, Fanny June Taylor Dunham, and her father, Albert Dunham, were musical. In her earliest memories Katherine can see them sitting together on Sunday evenings, playing musical duets. She still remembers how happy she felt when she heard her father play his guitar and how her mother's hair shone in the lamplight. But that is about all she can remember about her mother, for Fanny June Taylor Dunham died before Katherine was three.

Fanny was many years older than Albert Dunham, who was her second husband. She was first married to a Russian Jewish man. They had five children before he died. Because Fanny was very light-skinned and her husband was white, these children were also very light-skinned. They were grown up by the time Fanny married Albert Dunham, a black man, and started a second family.

That second family would consist of two children. Albert, Jr., was born first. Four years later, on June 22, 1909,

Katherine arrived. Both had medium-brown skin, and so in some ways they faced a tougher life than their older half brothers and sisters right from the start.

When Albert and Katherine were born, their parents were living in Glen Ellyn, Illinois. Fanny Dunham's first husband had left her an inheritance, and Albert and she had built a house before the children were born. Fanny bought property in a white section of the town, and because she was so light-skinned no one paid much attention. Work on the house began, and neighbors thought at first that the black man who came with Fanny to see how the work was going was someone who worked for her. The frame was up and the windows were in place when the neighbors found out that the black man was Fanny's husband. Not long after that a bomb exploded on the Dunham property. All it did was shatter one of the windows. But Albert Dunham realized there might be more bombs if he did not take a stand. He had every right to build a house and live wherever he wanted to, and he was going to protect that right.

There was a toolshed near the house. Albert took a double-barreled shotgun and stayed in that shed every night until the house was finished. No more bombs went off on the Dunham property.

All this happened about a year before Katherine was born. But for years afterward the relatives talked about it so much that she felt as if she had lived through that time, too. She learned very early that her father was a brave man. At the time, she did not know about racism. All she knew was that if someone threatens your house, you must be brave and protect it.

Sadly, the Dunham family was not to enjoy the new home for long. When Katherine was three and Albert seven, their mother became very ill and died. Her young husband was left with two small children, and he did not have a job. When he did get work, it was sales work. Traveling from town to town selling suiting goods, he would not be able to take care of his family. So Albert and Katherine went to live with their Aunt Lulu in Chicago.

Lulu Dunham lived in a cold-water flat in a run-down apartment house on the city's slum-ridden South Side, in an area called Mecca Flats. The bathroom down the hall was shared with other tenants, and so was the kitchen. If you wanted to keep food in the refrigerator you put your name on it and hoped other people would respect your property. Aunt Lulu was a beautician who had once worked out of her home, but she had lost her license to run a business in the flat, so now she had to go to her clients' homes.

The Chicago part of the Dunham family was not just musical but theatrical as well. Not far away from Aunt Lulu lived Aunt Clara and Uncle Arthur Dunham and their daughter Irene. Uncle Arthur was a voice coach and choral leader, and both his wife and daughter were aspiring singers and actresses. When Albert and Katherine arrived in Chicago to live with Aunt Lulu, Uncle Arthur and his family were putting the finishing touches on *Minnehaha*, a musical show about the American Indian princess who was celebrated in Henry Wadsworth Longfellow's poem, "The Song of Hiawatha." Three-year-old Katherine was fascinated by the people dancing around in feathers and war paint. She wanted to dance, too. But Aunt Clara sent her away, saying she was too young. The show, which opened at the Monogram Theatre soon after, did not last long enough for Katherine to get to see it. But she would get to see many other shows.

Not long after Albert and Katherine arrived, the question arose as to what to do with the children when Aunt Lulu was out at her clients' homes. Albert was older and would be in school most of the time. But Katherine was only three and needed looking after. It was decided that her cousin Irene would do that. Lulu would leave money for lunch and for coal for the small grate each day, and Irene would take care of Katherine and see that she was fed and kept warm.

But Irene was stage-struck, and she saw an opportunity to get to all the shows she longed to see. Each day she would arrive at Aunt Lulu's and see her aunt off, promising to take good care of Katherine. Then, as soon as she thought it was safe, she would take the money Aunt Lulu had left for lunch and coal, dress Katherine to go out, and head for the Monogram or the Grand Theatre and the afternoon vaudeville shows. After the shows she would rush back to Aunt Lulu's flat, often carrying a sleeping Katherine. She would buy a bit of coal along the way and at Aunt Lulu's she would build a small fire in the grate and rush to and fro fanning the heat around so it would seem as if the fire had been burning all day.

Except for being hungry a lot, Katherine liked being taken care of by Irene. She was too young to appreciate the fact that she was seeing some of the great names on the black vaudeville circuit—singers Ethel Waters and Bessie Smith, dancers and comedians Buck and Bubbles and Cole and Johnson—but she did enjoy the excitement of the shows. She loved the singing and dancing, the bright costumes and the laughter and cheering and foot-stomping of the audiences. And because she was so little, the people who worked in the theaters and attended the shows paid her a great deal of attention. They would give her candy or some of the fried chicken they had brought along to eat, and so she really did not suffer all that much because Irene spent their lunch money on theater tickets. And she didn't mind not telling Aunt Lulu, because Irene said it was a secret, and Katherine loved secrets. All this went on for about a year until Fanny Weir decided to pay a visit to Aunt Lulu's.

Fanny Weir was Fanny June Taylor Dunham's daughter by her first marriage. She was grown and married and had children of her own, and she did not think much of the family her mother had married into the second time around. She thought even less of Albert Dunham for going off and leaving his two small children—her half brother and sister—with poor relatives on Chicago's South Side. She happened to arrive at a time when Aunt Lulu was out and just Albert and Katherine were home. She looked around the cold and bare apartment. She went down the hall and peered into the dirty common bathroom. She looked at the equally dirty common kitchen. Then she ordered Albert and Katherine to get ready to leave. Albert said they should wait for Aunt Lulu to come home, but Fanny had made up her mind that the sooner she got the children out of that horrible, filthy place the better.

Albert and Katherine were taken to their half sister Fanny's large, well-heated apartment where they ate regular meals, bathed nightly in an inside bathroom, and went to bed early. They did not huddle together for warmth at night, or feel hunger gnawing at their stomachs all the time. But they felt another kind of coldness and hunger that they had never felt with their poor relatives in Chicago. Their cousins, Fanny's children, made them feel as if they did not belong.

These cousins were light-skinned, like their mother and grandmother, and so they felt that they were better than Albert and Katherine. There was strong color-consciousness among blacks in those days. Blacks as a race were treated as second-class citizens by the white population, but light-skinned blacks found life a little easier, for whites tended to treat better those who looked more like them—light-skinned people with wavy hair. This same color prejudice was carried over into the black community itself. As a rule, the leaders of the black community—the ministers and teachers and heads of clubs and organizations—were light-skinned. Even if you were not a leader of anything, if you were light-skinned you thought yourself a little bit better than someone with darker skin. And so, ironically, Katherine's first direct experience with color prejudice came from her own family. She was too young to understand it very well, but she did know that because her skin was brown and her hair was tightly curled, she somehow did not belong in the Weir family. She wanted very much to go back to Aunt Lulu's.

Meanwhile, Aunt Lulu and Albert Dunham, Sr., had joined forces to get the children back, and the matter of who should have custody of Albert, Jr., and Katherine was taken to court. Both children were questioned by the judge. When four-year-old Katherine was asked what she did when Aunt Lulu was out, she cheerfully told him all about the trips to the vaudeville houses. Too late, she realized that this secret should have been kept from the judge as well as from Aunt Lulu. The judge did not approve of the children's returning to live with Aunt Lulu. He ruled that until Albert, Sr., could provide a proper home for his children, they were better off with the Weirs.

The children went back to Fanny's, and they were miserable. The only hope they had to hold on to was their father's promise that he would make a home for them and that soon they would be together again. Albert, Sr., did not like being told by a judge that he was not a proper father. He liked even less the idea that one of his wife's light-skinned and uppity older daughters was telling him he couldn't take care of his own children. Within a year, Albert Dunham had his children back.

Albert, Jr., was nine and Katherine was five when their father came to take them away from Fanny. He came with a small, pretty brown-skinned woman who stood very straight and stiff when she was introduced to Fanny but who smiled warmly when she saw the children. Her name was Annette Poindexter Dunham, and she was their new mother. Then Albert and Katherine, with their father and stepmother, together began a new life.

Albert, Sr., had saved up money and bought a dry-cleaning business in Joliet, Illinois, and he was determined to make it a success. He had only himself and his family to depend on, for all the property Fanny June had left when she died had been sold to pay the debts of her children by her first marriage. Albert, Sr., a dark-skinned man in a society where your value as a human being was judged by your complexion, wanted to show this society that he could do as well as any light-skinned Negro—maybe even better.

From the start, everyone was involved in the family business. Besides keeping house and caring for the children, Annette kept the accounts and did all the mending and clothing alterations. Albert, Jr., made pick-ups and deliveries and helped out around the store. Even Katherine had her chores. She helped to tag the clothes so they would be returned to their right owners, and she helped her stepmother around the house. It was a very busy household! Young Katherine had a basis for comparison, because it was the fourth household she had lived in during her five years.

She did not have many memories of her first home, but she did remember the peace and happiness of her parents' evening musical duets. There were no such duets in this household. In fact, her father never played the mandolin or the guitar anymore. He spent his evenings going over account books and talking to his wife about his plans to expand the business. He was kind to his children, but he was impatient with them, too, and he did not seem to have much time for fun.

Still, Albert, Jr., and Katherine had no desire to go back to Fanny's, or even to Aunt Lulu's. After years of not being part of a real family, they appreciated the security of belonging somewhere.

There were some happy times. As his business started to grow, Albert Dunham could no longer deliver all the clothes on foot or by buggy, even with the help of Albert, Jr., so he bought a delivery van and a horse named Lady Fern to pull it. Sometimes on Sundays he would hitch up Lady Fern and take the whole family on a picnic. And sometimes, when he took the horse out for exercise, he would take the children with him. When they were far enough away so Annette could not see them, they would race Lady Fern up and down the field, and everyone, including Lady Fern, would feel as if there was not a better place to be anywhere than in that field on that happy, fun-filled day.

As time went on, though, there were fewer and fewer days when fun, not work, would be most important. All Mr. Dunham could seem to think about was his business. He reasoned that the harder he and his family worked, the more successful the business would be. So he worked hard, and he worked his family hard. He seemed to forget that his children were just children. Albert, Jr., especially, had so many chores to do that he barely found time to do his homework. Katherine was not expected to do as much, of course, but after she started school she found that there was little time for anything besides work and school.

Katherine began her education at the nearby Beale School. It was predominantly white, because there were not many blacks in Joliet. But Katherine did not feel the sting of racism in those early years. She knew she was different. That fact had been made clear to her by her own relatives. But she had both black and white friends, and none of them seemed to care much about complexion. They were too busy sharing their love of sports and performing.

Katherine and her friends were always making up little plays, nagging their mothers for old clothing and materials with which to make costumes. Katherine was a natural leader. She was the one who usually organized the plays, and who insisted that there be a lot of singing and dancing. She also usually got to be the featured dancer. Her claim was based on experience. After all, she had been to many shows at the great black vaudeville theaters in Chicago. Her friends, who thought her Chicago years must have been very glamorous, could hardly argue with that kind of experience. But some of their parents would take a dimmer view of Katherine's ideas once they saw them in practice.

The Dunhams attended Brown's African Methodist Episcopal Church in Joliet. Although its congregation was not especially well-to-do, the people tried very hard to raise money for less fortunate people. In the late winter of 1919, the church people were trying to raise money for the work of Methodist missionaries in East Angola, in Africa. They held rummage sales and bake sales and church suppers. Nine-year-old Katherine took the missionary cause very seriously and wanted to help, too. So she came up with the idea of getting her friends together and offering an evening of entertainment at the church. The grown-ups thought this was a fine idea and were proud of Katherine for wanting to help raise money for the Lord's work.

Katherine chose her cast and began to rehearse them. She supervised every detail of the show, from costumes to make-up. She knew exactly what kind of show she wanted; she had decided that her show would be a cabaret.

Cabaret is a French word that means a café or restaurant with singing and dancing as entertainment. Since upstanding, churchgoing people like Albert and Annette Dunham certainly did not go to such places, young Katherine must have gotten the idea in her Chicago days. It may seem hard to believe that she could remember in almost exact detail a cabaret show she had been to when only three or four years old, but it appears that she did.

Everything about the show was a secret. Katherine didn't even tell her parents what she was planning. Every time they asked her how the show was coming along, she would only say, "Just wait. You'll see." All the children involved kept the secret, and so it was a complete shock to everyone in the audience at Brown's Church when on Wednesday, March 10th, the makeshift curtain went up to reveal what amounted to a nightclub setting.

The audience gasped. The small performers took this reaction as one of awe and joyfully began their program. They then presented a show full of the most "worldly" entertainment ever presented at a black church in Joliet. There were blues songs and jazz dancing and such a display of youthful energy that some of the church elders came near to fainting.

This was not what anyone had expected. The congregation was used to children's Christmas pageants, not nightclub floor shows. When the program was over, there was a lot of muttering from the elders. But some of the younger members of the congregation muttered back that it had been a pretty good show. Once the minister got over his shock, he remembered that the purpose of the show was to raise money for missionary work. It had done that. Thirty-two dollars had been collected, he informed the congregation. After that announcement, even the grumblers applauded. Still, ever after, there would be a lingering suspicion on the part of the more staid churchgoers that little Katie Dunham might be a bit "wild."

Of course Katherine was not wild at all. But she had a wonderful sense of herself. In spite of all the work she had to do at home, she never forgot that she had a family now and that she belonged. And if sometimes her parents were too busy to pay much attention to her, she always had her brother. Perhaps because the two children had only had each other for several years in their early lives, they were very close, even though there was four years' difference in their ages. Albert, Jr., felt protective toward Katherine and she looked up to him. They never felt the need to compete with one another.

Albert, Jr., was a better student than Katherine. From the start, he made good grades in both his school subjects and in conduct. Katherine, on the other hand, was not very good in arithmetic and science and whispered to her friends so much that she was always getting bad conduct marks. Her best scores were in music and athletics. Her teachers would remark about how coordinated and athletic she was.

Both Albert, Jr., and Katherine were popular at school, but Katherine was more outgoing. At Farragut Elementary School, which she attended after Beale School, the girls liked to organize secret societies. Instead of trying to join someone else's society, Katherine decided to form one of her own. And hers would have a more exciting name and symbol than any of the others.

Back when she was just three years old, Katherine had seen her Uncle Arthur and Aunt Clara and cousin Irene rehearsing for their short-lived production of *Minnehaha*. Ever since then she had been fascinated with American Indians. One Christmas her brother gave her a book on American Indians, and she had studied it from cover to cover. So when she decided to form her own secret society at school, she went to her Indian book for ideas. The symbol she liked best in the whole book was the "Eagle Eye"—a large, staring eye that in Indian lore was supposed to see all. She decided to call her society the Eagle Eye Society, and she set about making headbands for her group with the symbol on them. She got strips of red satin and on them she sewed beads in the shape of a large, staring eye. Then she passed these headbands out to all the girls who had agreed to join her society.

The other girls were delighted. The symbol Katherine had created was the most talked-about subject in school. By comparison, the symbols of the other societies seemed very dull and unimaginative. How could matching skirts and blouses compete with Eagle Eye headbands? School authorities decided that the headbands attracted too much attention, and eventually they said the girls couldn't wear them to school anymore. But while they were allowed to wear them, the girls felt very special. And after the school said they couldn't wear the headbands anymore, the special feeling continued. After all, how many other secret societies had caused so much excitement that their symbolic dress had been *banned*?

Young Katherine Dunham had spirit, and so did the rest

of her family. Her father kept on working to build up his business, and pretty soon he expanded it to include not just clothes-cleaning but carpet-cleaning, too. The whole family would remember the banner day when his new carpet-cleaning machine arrived. It was an expensive piece of equipment, and Albert, Sr., was as proud of it as he would have been of one of those newfangled horseless carriages (which he also intended to have one day). It mechanically beat out the dust and dirt from carpets and rugs, and soon it became known around the community as Albert Dunham's dust wheel. With the profits from his carpet-cleaning business, Albert Dunham was able to install electricity in both his shop and his home, and that caused his family to be the envy of a large portion of the rest of the community. Most people still used gas and kerosene to light their homes and electricity was a luxury they could not afford. Albert, Sr., was proud that he could have such a service.

His wife was proud of it, too. But she had a right to be, because she worked as hard as her husband did. Annette Poindexter Dunham worked so hard, in fact, that at times she became physically ill. But she rarely complained. She had been raised to be successful. She had become a school-teacher, which among blacks at that time was a highly respected profession. If she now directed her energies to account books instead of essay books, to mending and alter-ing clothes instead of correcting and changing ideas, she was still working toward something better. And she wasn't just a drone, like a worker bee in a hive, for she had outside inter-ests. She was very active in church affairs, even though her husband didn't think much of them.

The Dunham children also strived for success. Although they worked hard at the family business, they were not just worker-bees either. After the carpet-cleaning machine arrived, Albert, Jr., got the job of helping to fix it whenever it broke down. The machine broke down a lot and because Albert was small he could squeeze into the space his father created with a wooden plank and find the strap that had broken. Albert would splice the strap so the wheel would turn again. It was a dangerous job (Katherine would always go along and pray silently for her brother's safety), but doing it and all the other work just seemed to make Albert stronger in the world outside his family. He continued to do well at school and to be popular with his classmates. He had to sandwich his homework in between his duties in the shop, but he was named class valedictorian in his senior year. Even though he had little time to have fun with friends, in his senior year he was also elected class president.

Katherine, too, seemed to thrive on the busy life she led. By now she was helping her stepmother mend and alter the clothes, keep the accounts, and do the household chores (plus giving her brother moral support every time the dust wheel broke down). Instead of devoting whatever spare time she had to doing her homework, as Albert, Jr., did, she kept up a variety of friendships. And she continued to plan shows and make up skits and corral whoever she could into being an audience. Although they despaired over her work in most scholastic subjects, her teachers praised her in several areas: she seemed to have a natural talent for writing. While still in junior high, Katherine wrote a class poem and a story that were accepted and published in the national magazine *Child Life*. And there was no question about her athletic and dancing abilities. Her teachers said she really ought to take dancing lessons, and Katherine agreed with them. She loved writing, but she loved to dance even more.

"I think I was born interested in dance," Katherine says now. "As far back as I can remember, I was interested in motion. I wasn't interested in singing. I was choreographing. . . . I don't know where it came from. No one danced in my immediate family. In fact, it was considered something that nice, upstanding people didn't do. But there were those memories of the Chicago years. . . . All I know is that I was always thinking in terms of rhythm and motion. I danced because I had to."

So, she went to her stepmother with the idea, and Annette approved. Then Annette broached the subject to her husband, and he didn't think much of it. To his mind, the only sure road to success was the road of business, which is why the fact that Albert, Jr., had been elected president of his class and class valedictorian did not impress him as much as it perhaps should have. At the same time, his ability to pay for dancing lessons for his daughter was a sure sign of his own success. Katherine got her dancing lessons, but her father grumbled a little bit every time he paid the bill. He wanted to know what kind of future Katherine would get from taking dancing lessons.

 THREE

BY THE TIME KATHERINE WAS IN SIXTH GRADE, HER FA-
ther's business had become so successful that he was able to
buy a second-hand Studebaker automobile. It was his pride
and joy, and the talk of the neighborhood. Very few people
owned automobiles in those days. Now, instead of picking
up and delivering clothes in a wagon pulled by Lady Fern,
Albert Dunham proudly drove through the streets of Joliet
in a horseless carriage.

Albert, Jr., soon learned to drive the Studebaker because
his father wanted him to make pick-ups and deliveries in it.
But Katherine was surprised and overjoyed to learn that
she, too, would be taught to drive. Her father didn't like
having to take his wife to all her church activities, and he
decided that Katherine should learn to drive the car so she
could chauffeur her stepmother around instead. There was
no minimum legal age for driving then, and people did not
have to have driver's licenses. At the age of 12, Katherine
was driving, and in the summer of 1921 she and her stepmother even took a trip to visit Annette's relatives in Alton,
Illinois.

On the way, they stopped in St. Louis. The city had a very large black community, and in that community was a very famous street lined with vaudeville houses and dance halls and restaurants. Chouteau Street was famous for its fried fish, and Annette and Katherine wanted to try some.

Katherine had never seen anything like Chouteau Street. Although she remembered Mecca Flats in Chicago as a pretty glamorous place, she was quite sure it did not have the same sense of glamour and style and gaiety. The men and women dressed in bright, flashy clothes and wore lots of jewelry. They were also very open in showing their affection for one another, which was something Annette and Katherine were not used to seeing. They had both been brought up very strictly, and Katherine would always remember Annette's mother, Grandma Poindexter, saying: "Twenty-six years and three days, and thirteen children! And never once, mind you, did Ed Poindexter ever see me *even in a nightshirt!*"

On Chouteau Street there was music and singing everywhere, and Katherine responded to the rhythms and spirit of this strange, exciting place. It was such a different world from hers, and it appealed to her greatly. Years later she would recall that during that visit to St. Louis "there began a possession by the blues . . . deeper than prayer and closer to the meaning of life than anything else . . . something people are supposed to know about and don't look at, or knew a long time ago and lost." And the fried fish was just as delicious as its reputation had promised. Katherine would later describe it as a kind of ritual food taken on her initiation into a new way of life.

But that new way of life was many years away for young Katherine Dunham. The wonderful summer trip over, she and her stepmother returned to Joliet, Illinois, and their staid and hardworking existence.

Katherine entered high school that fall. Her brother Albert had graduated in June and was starting junior college. He'd had a fine high school career. All the teachers said he was one of the most brilliant students ever to attend the school. Katherine knew that if the teachers expected her to get the kinds of grades Albert, Jr., had, they were going to be disappointed. But she also knew that she would excel in other ways and leave her own lasting impression.

In high school, Katherine enjoyed having a greater range of courses to choose from, and more extracurricular activities. She took as many dance and gym classes as she could, and practiced hockey and basketball in the hope of making the girls' teams. The clubs in high school were not the silly secret organizations of grade school. They consisted of groups of students who shared common interests and who wanted to excel in what they liked to do. The one Katherine wanted to belong to was the Terpsichorean Club, named after Terpsichore, the Greek goddess of dancing. "It was devoted to interpretive dance," she recalls, "and we'd go around with scarves and be woods fairies, and I was upset because, being new, I had to be a brownie." The club held dance recitals, and members of the club were always the soloists at the school's annual spring dance recital. Katherine admired these skillful dancers. At the school recital the following spring she was especially impressed with a soloist who did the famous Russian *hopak*. Back at home that night, Katherine tried folding her arms and squatting on the floor and thrusting out one leg in front of her and then the other. She wanted to learn how to do this spirited dance, but it was not part of the school's dance curriculum. So she asked her father for private lessons and he agreed to pay for them, even though he grumbled a lot.

Albert, Sr., grumbled a lot, too, about his son's college bills. In his view, college was a waste of time. He had never gone to college, and look how successful he was. Even worse, Albert, Jr., was not interested in taking college commercial courses that would at least prepare him to take over the family dry-cleaning business. No, Albert, Jr., was studying philosophy!

The disagreement over Albert, Jr.'s, future led to a great deal of tension in the Dunham household. Once, when Albert, Jr., was studying in his room at night, his father actually went down to the basement and turned off the electricity—and was proud of himself for doing it.

There were other sources of tension. Business at the dry-cleaning shop was falling off. Probably the main reason was the tightening of the color bar in Joliet. The end of World War I saw a large northern migration of blacks from the South, and as more blacks arrived whites began to resent them and fear that they were somehow "taking over." Albert Dunham had had enough experience with white racism to see this change in attitude, but apparently he did not accept it. He decided that his family would simply have to work harder. While he went out after more business, his wife would have to spend more time at the store, and that meant that Katherine would have to take on extra household duties. She had less time for dancing and sports, but she just worked harder at what she wanted to do and managed to secure an invitation to join the Girl's Athletic League at school. Dancing and playing sports were the only ways she had to relieve some of the tension that built up in her, over what was happening at home.

Then her father decided that his business was not secure enough for him to depend on it entirely and that he should start investing in real estate. From now on, he told his fam-

ily, every spare penny would be put aside to buy property—
and he meant *every spare penny*. Annette Dunham had to
cut back on the quality of the food she bought, and there
was no more money for new curtains and other small
household luxuries. For the children, there were no more
new clothes, even when they really needed them. Meanwhile, everyone was expected to work harder than ever.

Annette Dunham did not like this situation at all, and she
said so. She and her husband began to quarrel a lot, and
then he started hitting her. After one big fight, Annette left
home. She returned after Albert, Sr., promised that things
would be different if she would come back. For a while
things were different, and Katherine and Albert, Jr., tried
especially hard not to create any tensions because they had
been miserable with Annette gone. But after a time the
same old problems came back to the surface of life in the
Dunham household.

By this time Albert, Jr., was in his second year of junior
college, and he was determined to go on to senior college.
He had applied for a scholarship to the University of Chicago, and he was praying that he would get it. His father
was furious at him. If Albert went off to Chicago, who
would help him at the dry-cleaning store? His son had not
turned out as he had hoped at all. Instead of books on business and real estate, he read books on philosophy. Instead of
trying to figure out new ways to make money, he played the
cello.

One afternoon while Albert, Jr., was playing his cello,
Albert, Sr., lost his temper. He struck his son. Albert, Jr.,
had been hit by his father before and never fought back. But
this time all the resentment he'd been feeling for years came
out. He struck back at his father, and the two fought as if
they wanted to kill each other. Annette and Katherine tried

to stop them, but they could not. They finally had to get the young worker from the shop downstairs to separate the two men.

Shaking with rage, Albert, Sr., ordered his son to leave home and never come back. Without a word, Albert, Jr., went upstairs to pack his belongings. Annette pleaded with her husband and stepson to change their minds, but neither one would listen to her. Carrying a cardboard box full of clothes and an armful of books, Albert, Jr., stormed out of the house, brushing past Katherine without a word.

Katherine stood frozen in horror. She couldn't believe Albert was leaving her. They had never been separated before in their whole lives. She wanted to go with him, but she knew he would have a tough enough time making it on his own without having the added burden of a little sister. Still, she couldn't see how she could possibly continue to live in that house without Albert.

For Annette Dunham, the fight and Albert, Jr.'s, leaving home were just about the last straw, and not many months after Albert left, Annette announced that she was leaving too. Katherine did not want to be left alone with her father, and she begged to go with her stepmother. Annette and Albert worked out a curious future relationship, mostly for Katherine's sake. Annette and Katherine would move out of the house and find a place of their own. But Annette would still do the mending and alterations on the clothes, and Katherine would still work in the shop after school and on weekends. And because Katherine was his real daughter, Albert would continue to make the major decisions about her life.

At least he was no longer a constant presence in Katherine's life, and that caused her to feel a lot less tense. She was happy living with her stepmother in the rooms they rented in another section of town. She did not like working in her father's store, but at least she could look forward to leaving at the end of the day and going home to a place where there were no arguments and fights.

Albert, Jr., visited whenever he could. By this time he was in Chicago, for his scholarship to the University of Chicago had come through. His tuition and books were paid for by the scholarship, but he had to work for his own room and board. It was hard finding part-time jobs that paid enough, and he was forced to work so many hours that he could not take as many courses as he wanted to. He was too proud, and too resentful, to ask his father for help. When Annette brought up the subject of Albert with her husband, the older man flatly refused to talk about it. So Annette and Katherine scrimped in order to help out Albert, Jr. They were used to scrimping anyway, and saving every penny to help out young Albert was a lot more satisfying than doing it so Albert, Sr., could invest in real estate.

In spite of all her family problems, Katherine had been able to put such things behind her and get as much enjoyment as possible from school. She was popular with her classmates, and she excelled in sports and dance even though she had less time to practice than many other girls who were interested in the same things. She had always been well-coordinated, and in junior high school she had begun to grow tall. By the time she was in eleventh grade she was about 5'6", and she was the center on the girls' basketball team. She was also elected president of the Girl's Athletic League and won the membership in the Terpsichorean Club she had wanted since entering high school.

In her high school, Katherine was unique. Most girls pursued either sports or dance, not both. But for Katherine the combination of the two was perfectly natural. Both skills required coordination. If dance needed grace, it also needed stamina and strength. And if stamina and strength were important in a game like basketball, grace was important, too. On graduation from high school, Katherine knew that she had left her own mark on the school, just as her brother had.

Also like her brother, Katherine went to junior college after high school. Her father paid her tuition, because even though she no longer lived in his house she was a dutiful daughter. She still worked in the dry-cleaning store and still asked her father for permission to go to parties or on visits to her mother's relatives in Chicago. She was still very much under his thumb, and he kept his thumb down pretty hard.

In no area was Albert Dunham more strict than in his ideas about dating. Nice girls did not go out on dates, he said. He allowed Katherine to go to church socials, or to dances with a group of girls. But she was never to go with, or leave with, a boy and she was always to be home early. In her first high school years, Katherine did not mind these restrictions. She was too busy to think about boys. Nor was she all that interested in boys in her last high school years. But she was beginning to feel funny about not being able to go out on dates when all her friends could. And she did not like the idea that her father did not trust her, for she had never given him any reason for distrust.

By the time she entered junior college, Katherine was beginning to resent her father's dominance. In this area, her stepmother was not very sympathetic. Aside from the fact that Annette Dunham had been brought up very strictly herself, she respected the fact that Albert, Sr., was Katherine's real father and that she was not Katherine's real mother. So when it came to major decisions about Katherine, she bowed to his wishes. Sometimes, she thought he was too harsh and uncompromising, but she tried not to let Katherine see how she felt. She did not want to get caught in the middle between the man and his daughter.

Albert, Jr., was very sympathetic. After years of struggling to work and go to school both, he had finally been granted a full scholarship at the University of Chicago. It paid not just for his tuition and books but also for his room and board. He was proud that he had been able to make it on his own, and he encouraged his sister to try to do the same. "Come to Chicago," he urged. "I'll help you."

On the surface, Katherine liked the idea of going to Chicago. But she had a lot of misgivings. She did not feel as if she had ever had quite the same degree of determination as Albert, Jr., had. He had seemed to know exactly what he wanted to be and do. She did not. She knew what she liked, of course, but she did not have the same definite dreams about her future. She did not think she could ever just pack up and leave as Albert had.

On top of that, the girl who had always seemed so sure of herself was having doubts about her ability to act properly in social situations. She was learning that the skills you needed to play basketball or dance well or have a good time at a church social where you knew everyone were not all that you needed at a party where you didn't know anyone at all. She had been to such parties while visiting her mother's relatives in Chicago, and she had not enjoyed them. She had been a wallflower, watching other girls act in a relaxed and natural way and wondering how they did it, sitting on the sidelines while others did what she loved to do—dance. When a boy did ask her to dance at these parties, she felt as if she were made out of wood. And her voice seemed to stop working altogether. How in the world could she go to Chicago to live when she couldn't even manage to enjoy a Chicago party?

But her brother kept pressing. In her second year of junior college, Katherine received an application form for a part-time library job in Chicago, and later, a letter saying she was scheduled to take the entrance exam for admission to the university. Albert was setting her future in motion for her, since she didn't seem to be able to make her own decisions. After stalling for a while, Katherine filled out the job application and later passed the university entrance exam. But she was still not sure she ought to leave Joliet, where she knew people and felt comfortable. In the end, it was not really Katherine, but her father, who made her decision, just as he had for Albert, Jr.

In her second year at junior college, Katherine met William Booker, who was new to Joliet. They shared common interests, like sports, and they began to meet regularly at school. But that was the extent of their relationship, for every time Bill Booker asked her to a dance or a game she had to refuse. She was made to do so by her father. She was also told she could not accept Bill's basketball letter. Katherine felt terrible about having to say no to even the most innocent invitations from Bill, but she was afraid to go against her father. Bill was not put off. He saw Katherine whenever he could, and both hoped for a time when things would be different.

But toward the end of the year, Bill got two tickets to the state championship basketball game, and both of them wanted so badly to go to it together that Bill decided to take matters into his own hands. He would visit Mr. Dunham personally and ask his permission to take Katherine to the game.

The next thing Katherine knew, her father was at

Annette's home, raging through the door to find Katherine, calling her terrible names and accusing her of being a tramp. Katherine was so shocked she couldn't say anything. But then her father hit her, and in an instant she found her voice and all the words she had thought but had not said over the years. All her anger and resentment seemed to pour out of her, and for a moment, at least, it was Albert Dunham, Sr., who was speechless. The next morning, Katherine left for Chicago. Like her brother years before, she just could not be around her father anymore. She didn't like leaving Annette, but she knew it was time to start a new life. She was 18 years old and had never been on a date, didn't know what she wanted to do nor where she wanted to be. All she knew was that she did not want to be anywhere near her father.

FOUR

YEARS LATER, KATHERINE WOULD DESCRIBE HERSELF AT that time:

She had reached her full growth of five feet six and three-quarter inches, weighed one hundred and twenty-three pounds, and had dark brown eyes and dark brown hair, with a streak of auburn buried in the middle. Her skin was a light brown, so tinged with green that in a strong light—as for instance, in the spotlights focused on her in her later stage career—she might appear startlingly pale. She found her features exceedingly plain and, because she had no hope of equalling her brother's scholastic brilliance, foresaw no exceptional future for herself.

Albert was waiting for her when she arrived at the train station in Chicago, and he did much to help her during her first few weeks in the city. Although she had been accepted at the university, her grades were not high enough to win her a scholarship. Albert helped her arrange for a student loan. He also helped her to understand the realities of being black in a white society.

Katherine was no stranger to racism. She'd heard many times the story of how her father had guarded his new house from bombers who did not want a black in their neighborhood. She had felt racism from her own lighter-skinned relatives when she was very small. Later, after the family had been reunited in Joliet, she had experienced the feeling of being different in predominantly white neighborhoods and schools, and it had not taken her too long to realize that one reason her father had worked himself and his family so hard was that he wanted to show he was just as good as any white man.

When she was in high school she had objected to some of the songs the music teacher taught his students to sing—the lyrics were about lazy or shiftless or stupid black people. Annette Dunham had gone to the principal about that, and the music teacher had been demoted to band leader and the objectionable songs had been banned.

Around the same time, Albert, Jr., had been denied election as president of his class in junior college because he was black. But these instances of outright racism had been comparatively rare in Katherine's life. As a rule, blacks and whites in Joliet got along fairly well together, as long as the blacks did not overstep the invisible bounds that white society had put around them.

Katherine had gotten the idea, though, that things would be different in Chicago, where there were so many black people and where the people, black and white, were supposed to be more sophisticated. And so it came as a shock to her to find out that she had been hired for the part-time library job because the people at the library thought she was white. When she showed up for work, schedules were quickly shuffled around so she would not share her lunch hour with anyone else, and duties were quickly changed so that she found herself alone in a back room doing cataloguing all day. Back at Albert's that night, she said she wanted to quit, but he reminded her that quitting would not be very realistic. It might solve the current problem, but it would create a lot of others. She needed the job, and until she found another one she had better swallow her pride.

Twenty-two-year-old Albert had been very successful in Chicago. Not only had he done well in his studies, earning scholarships to help him get his bachelor of arts degree and go on for his master's degree, but also he had made many friends and gotten involved in a lot of activities. He helped Katherine to ease herself into the big-city world and to make her own friends, and after some shyness in the beginning she never became the wallflower she was afraid she would be in Chicago, or anywhere else outside Joliet.

Chicago could be a very exciting place for an intelligent and artistic black person in the 1920s. That was a time when many blacks were moving up to the northern cities from the South, swelling the black populations of those cities and giving those populations a sense of pride and power in their sheer numbers. At the same time, certain white artists and writers and rich people seemed suddenly to "discover" the Negro. Blacks were seen as somehow more exotic and unspoiled and natural than whites, and all of a sudden their music and dancing and writing became sought after by these whites. Blacks were suddenly very "in." This trend seemed to be strongest in New York—the whole era is called the "Harlem Renaissance"—but it touched other cities with large black populations, too.

By the time Katherine arrived in Chicago, Albert and some of his friends had started the Cube Theatre as "an independent venture of students and artists interested in all forms of modern art." It was an integrated group, and ten years earlier could probably not have existed. Now, young white people in the arts, at least, believed they could learn much from the black experience. The existence of this group helped to offset in Katherine's mind the racism she encountered at the library. She had her first acting experience on a real stage in this theater, and through it she would also meet people who would help her in her first attempts at a career.

Katherine had gone to Chicago mainly to get away from her father and get closer to Albert. She had no idea what subject she wanted to get a degree in. She loved to dance, but the university offered no degree in dance, so she took courses in a variety of subjects and dancing lessons on the side. She took tap dancing lessons for a while, and then ballet classes. Frances Taylor, a black girl from Hartford, Connecticut, whom she had met through the Cube Theatre, took these lessons with her, and the two became roommates and best friends.

Albert liked Frances, too. She was very bright and had won a full, four-year scholarship to the university, and at first he just liked having discussions with her. He had no intention to marry because he had too many things to do. But then he won a foundation grant to study philosophy at Harvard, and his attitude changed. He asked Frances to marry him, and she accepted, and before Katherine could understand it all her brother and her best friend had gone off to Cambridge, Massachusetts.

Left alone, Katherine threw herself into dance. Her ballet teacher, Madame Ludmila Speranzeva, did not just teach dance steps; she taught her students to act out stories in their dancing. Katherine excelled at this, and she began to dream about leaving the library job and opening a dance school of her own.

Ruth Page and Mark Turbyfill, two ballet dancers with the Chicago Opera Company who were also involved in the Cube Theatre, encouraged her. In fact, one offered to pay for her studio space and the other offered to teach free of charge. Excitedly, Katherine rented studio space and advertised for students, and in early 1930 when she was barely 21 years old, she opened her school. A few months earlier, the New York Stock Market had crashed and the Great Depression had begun, but young Katherine Dunham did not realize that these events over which she had no control would affect her school.

From the beginning, Katherine wanted her school to be more than the ordinary ballet school. Through Albert and her experiences in Chicago, she had come to feel that black people had a special style. Her dance friends agreed and suggested that she try to bring that out in the dances she taught. They also suggested that she ought to emphasize this new type of dancing by calling her group of students the Ballet Nègre (Negro Ballet). So Katherine began not only to teach steps but also to choreograph dances, planning individual and group movements on the stage that would bring out this special style.

In 1931 Katherine and her school got what she believed was a big break. They were invited to perform at the annual Beaux Arts Ball, which showcased new talent. Katherine choreographed a special dance called "Negro Rhapsody" and the performance, the first act of the evening, was very well received. Katherine was thrilled and sure that the appearance would bring publicity and financial support for her school. Unfortunately, all the acts that followed were equally well received. Katherine had wanted "Negro Rhapsody" to be the sensation of the evening, and perhaps she had built up her students' expectations that it would be. When it wasn't, they were as disappointed as she.

Things seemed to go downhill from there. The students began to drop out. Katherine's first and only backers, Ruth Page and Mark Turbyfill, went back to their own careers, not because they had stopped believing in Katherine but because they had given her as much help as they could for the time being. Without rent money and someone to share the teaching load, and with few remaining students, Katherine was forced to close her school.

On the rebound, or so it seems, she married a fellow dancer named Jordis McCoo. Both were struggling to make it as dancers, and they did not have much time to be together. Jordis worked nights in the post office. Katherine spent days going to school and to dance classes. She also sought a way to reopen her dance school. For a short time she joined forces with a friend named Ruth Attaway, who taught drama, and operated a combined dancing-drama school, but this school did not last very long either. Winter came, and the two women could not afford to heat the large stable they were using as a studio. A sympathetic friend with mechanical knowledge connected the stable's gas pipes to the street gas main, but the police soon came and put a stop to that. Once again, Katherine had no dancing school.

But Katherine continued her own dancing lessons. She was willing to go without just about everything to keep them up. The more she learned the more certain she was that she wanted to dance above everything else. But there was a terrible conflict inside her. She kept hearing her father's voice saying, "What kind of future is there in dance?" and even though she didn't like him she sometimes found herself admitting that what he said might be true. She had already found out that it was tough making a go of a dancing school. But just when she was despairing most and thinking about giving up and becoming a schoolteacher after all, she had an exciting experience.

One day she heard that Dr. Robert Redfield, a professor in the university's Department of Anthropology, was going to give a lecture on the bits and pieces of African culture that had survived in the New World after slavery. She went to hear this lecture, and she came away filled with excitement. Dr. Redfield had talked about African survivals in many areas of Negro-American culture, but what had interested Katherine was what he had said about dance. Popular dances in America, like the Lindy Hop and the Cakewalk and the Black Bottom, could be traced back to Africa!

Katherine had long felt that black dancing had a particular style about it. Now she knew why. These dances had roots in African dances. She wished she could go to Africa and find out just how the dances of the two cultures did connect. But since there didn't seem to be any way to do that, she decided that she could at least put what she had learned into her own dancing. And she decided that she could teach other young black dancers that they had a long tradition to be proud of.

Katherine's own teacher, Ludmila Speranzeva, was excited about the idea, too. She also knew that Katherine wasn't just some silly girl who took dancing because it was a way to learn gracefulness. Madame Speranzeva recognized in Katherine the same commitment she herself had to the art of dance, and so she offered Katherine the use of her own studio for yet another dancing school. Katherine accepted at once. She called her new group the Negro

Dance Group because she thought perhaps the name of the last group, Ballet Nègre, had been too exotic.

Unfortunately, this new name put off black parents just as much as the French name had. In the minds of these parents, the name Negro Dance Group meant that their children would learn souped-up versions of the Lindy Hop and the Black Bottom. Worse still, it might mean that their daughters would be taught to dance like African savages.

Most black people were not proud of their African heritage in those days. The majority of books published in the United States talked about Africans as savages who lived in grass huts and didn't wear enough clothes and had always been ruled by the white man. In those days, if you really wanted to know about Africa, you had to go to a big library and find some musty old book that hardly anyone had taken out for years to find out the truth. Only in such a book could you find out that there had been great societies in Africa, with rich and powerful kings, more civilized than those in Europe at the same time. Katherine Dunham had started reading those musty old books. She didn't need them to convince her that modern popular dances started by blacks had their roots in Africa. She had felt it all along. She was excited by the idea. She did not realize that many other blacks would not share her excitement, would not even want to read the old books and find out that she had a reason to be excited.

Katherine's third school was a failure, too. This time it was not because it did not get enough attention and not because it had no heat. This time it was because the black parents who paid tuition for their children to attend the school did not want their daughters to learn primitive dances. They wanted them to learn ballet, so they would be graceful and "refined."

Katherine felt badly when her third school was forced to close. But this time she had something else to think about that gave her hope. Her friend Ruth Page had composed a ballet that was just what Katherine had been dreaming could be done. Based on a folktale from Martinique, an island in the Lesser Antilles off Venezuela, it told of a devil woman who lured men to their death. Ruth asked Katherine to dance the major role, and Katherine's husband, Jordis McCoo, got to be part of the chorus of dancing men. The ballet was staged at the Chicago Opera House.

Katherine's father and stepmother attended the performance together. Albert Dunham's dry-cleaning business and his real estate plans had both suffered as a result of the growing Depression. But instead of making him more miserly and driven to succeed, these business reverses had caused him to sit back and take a long, hard look at his life. He realized that putting all his time and energy into making money had been foolish, because one can never be prepared for things like economic depressions. He had driven away his wife and his children, and yet they were the very people who would have stood by him if he had given them half a chance. He had talked Annette into moving back into their house. And now he was trying to make up for all the hurt he had caused his children. It was a good time to make up with Albert, Jr., for Albert and his wife, Frances, were expecting the first Dunham grandchild. A son named Kaye Lawrence Dunham was born in September 1933. Also, Albert, Jr., was continuing to prove that he was a brilliant scholar and had made the right choice for his own future. After getting his doctorate in philosophy, he had been hired as a professor at Howard University in Washington, D.C.

It was also an excellent time for Albert, Sr., to make up

with Katherine. Just having her father and stepmother come together to see her dance made the evening a joyous one. But there were other wonderful things to come out of her debut with the Chicago Opera Company.

The ballet, which was called *La Guiablesse*, got very good reviews in the newspapers, and so did the dancing of its star, Katherine Dunham. As a result of her performance, she was chosen to hire and train 150 young black dancers for a program to be presented at the 1934 Chicago World's Fair. It also brought her to the attention of Mrs. Alfred Rosenwald Stern and the Rosenwald Fund.

FIVE

THE JULIUS ROSENWALD FUND HAD ESTABLISHED THE MUSEUM of Science and Industry in Chicago in 1929. It had also given large contributions to the University of Chicago. But its main reason for being was to help black people, especially in education. Altogether, the Fund helped to build 5,000 schools for blacks in 15 southern states. It also gave fellowships to individual black students so they could continue their education.

By the time Katherine Dunham came into contact with the Rosenwald Fund, she wanted very much to continue her education. She wanted to study anthropology and find out more about the peoples of the world and their cultures. She especially wanted to study the dances of black people and to trace those dances back to their roots in Africa. Ever since she had heard Dr. Redfield lecture on the subject at the university, she had been excited to learn all she could about black dancing. She had taken as many courses in anthropology as she could and was completely absorbed by the field. But she had noticed that these courses paid very little attention to dance, and by now she was convinced that dance wasn't just entertainment, it was an important social act.

People danced to communicate. They danced in a shared tradition. The dances of a culture were as important as their other customs. But few anthropologists had really studied the dances of various cultures and those that had did not study them closely enough.

I would wonder why reports on American Indian dancing, for example, were so disappointing. And of course the answer was that these anthropologists were not dancers. They could not participate, and so they could not really understand. They did their best work studying things they could participate in—like men's puberty rites—they could participate in these rites because they were men. But dancing is different. It's very hard to describe, and it is almost impossible to understand unless you are a dancer.

Katherine realized that she would have to find out about the dances of various cultures herself. So, when she learned that the Rosenwald people were interested in her, she decided to ask the Scholarship Fund to give her a grant so she could find out what she wanted to know.

The members of the Scholarship Committee of the Rosenwald Fund listened to many pleas for support each year. They were used to seeing hopeful young black students talk earnestly about their plans for study and present books and manuscripts and college papers as evidence that they were serious about their work. But Katherine Dunham arrived for her interview without this kind of evidence. When the chairman of the committee asked her to explain why she wanted its financial support, Katherine said it was hard to explain in words. It would be much easier if she could show the committee what she wanted to do. The chairman told her to go ahead.

Katherine stood up, and before the eyes of the astonished committee she took off the jacket and skirt of her suit and removed her shoes. Dressed now in her black dancing leotard and tights, she began an exhibition of basic ballet steps. Then suddenly, she launched into a wild display that was her own idea of an African tribal dance. While the committee recovered from its shock, she put her suit and shoes back on and began to explain what it was she wanted to do.

She wanted to go where people still danced such ancient tribal dances. She wanted to find out why they danced this way. She wanted to learn how these dances had survived in the dancing of American blacks. Most of all, she explained, she wanted to understand dance as it began originally. American dancing was stilted and inhibited, and most Americans seemed to dance mostly because it was the thing to do. She believed that the original purpose of dancing, or at least the original effect of it, was to make people feel a part of the community. She emerged from the meeting with the feeling that she had impressed the committee. In fact, one member had suggested that the West Indies would be an excellent place for her to go to study. And she had agreed that it would. But all she could do was wait for their decision.

While she was waiting and hoping for good news from the Rosenwald Fund, Katherine received some bad family news. Albert, Jr., had suffered a mental breakdown and was in St. Elizabeth's Hospital in Washington, D.C. This news was a real blow to Katherine. Her brother had always seemed so sure of who he was and what he wanted to be. She had looked to him as a model of self-assurance. Only recently had she come to feel sure of what she wanted to do and be. Now, she realized that this was no guarantee of happiness.

But there was no turning back. In January 1935 she received word that she had been granted a fellowship to go to the West Indies. At the age of 25 she had at last found her direction and people who believed in her enough to support her in pursuing her chosen path.

Once she had won the Rosenwald Fund grant, Katherine did not just pack up and take off for the West Indies, although that is what she wanted to do. The older and wiser people of the Rosenwald Scholarship Committee knew that if she was going to make the most of her chance to travel she would have to be fully prepared. Of the $2,400 grant Katherine received, $500 was for tuition and living expenses from March to June 1935 while she studied under Dr. Melville Herskovits, chairman of the Department of African Studies at Northwestern University in Chicago.

Dr. Herskovits is dead now, but he is still considered one of the greatest African scholars who ever lived. Nowadays, many colleges and universities have African Studies departments and fine scholars, but back in 1935 there were hardly any such departments. And there were hardly any professors like this white, Jewish man whose books and other writings remain required reading for anyone who wants to trace the African heritage of the black peoples of the world.

At first, Katherine was impatient with the work she had to do under Dr. Herskovits. She wanted to get out into "the field." But she soon learned that the professor had many important things to teach her. He taught her that she couldn't expect to learn much if she studied dance and nothing else. To really learn about the dances she had to learn about the whole culture—what the people wore and what they ate and how they moved and spoke. He also taught her that if she wanted scholars to respect her work she would have to learn how to make proper reports. She could not rely on just her memory or her notes. She would have to make records of her findings—photographs and tape recordings. To do this, she had to learn how to operate and take care of cameras and tape recorders.

She had to learn also how to enter and be accepted in a new culture. She could not just barge in and tell people she was going to study them. She had to understand that the people would be suspicious of her and that she would have to show them that she could be trusted. If she failed to do that, they would not accept her; her trip would be wasted because she would learn no more than an ordinary tourist. And finally, she had to learn how to take care of herself, because she was going into an entirely different world. Years before, she may have thought that going from Joliet to Chicago was going from one world to another, but at least both those worlds had the same food and the same conveniences like feather beds and toilets and hospitals. In the West Indies there were foods she had never eaten, a climate she had never lived in, diseases she had never heard of, and very few feather beds, porcelain toilets or hospitals. She had to learn about medicines and what ailments they were for, what kinds of clothes were best for a tropical climate, how to keep her note paper and film and tapes from being destroyed by the abundant moisture. It was not long before Katherine forgot her impatience to get on with her trip. In fact, as June arrived, she wished she could spend many more months studying under Dr. Herskovits. She wondered if this three-month crash course in anthropology field work had prepared her enough for this exciting adventure that now seemed to be a little bit frightening, too.

In nervous moments, Katherine wondered how she could possibly gain acceptance among the people she wanted to study. She had learned from Dr. Herskovits that it was not enough to have some romantic idea of these people. She might want to study them, but they might not want to be studied. If she was not careful she could wind up as a tolerated outsider, and all she had learned about the techniques of field work would be useless.

In July 1935 the young woman whose former idea of a big trip had been to go to St. Louis, Missouri, took off for the West Indies. She traveled overland from Chicago to New York. In New York Harbor, she boarded the first ship she had ever set foot on. It was a Royal Netherlands ship, and though it was small by oceangoing vessel standards, it seemed huge to her. As the ship drew away from the shore, she found herself looking back at the Manhattan skyline and crying, which was silly, she knew, since this was the first time she had ever seen it. But at that moment, it represented home, and she was leaving it behind.

That evening she dressed formally for dinner, as she had read people on shipboard did, and felt silly again. There were only about five other passengers on the ship, and they had not bothered to dress up. Fortunately, the other passengers were very understanding, but Katherine realized that her lessons on other cultures were not going to come to her just in the West Indies. She started learning long before she reached the small village in Northeast Jamaica called Accompong where Dr. Herskovits had recommended that she study the culture of the descendants of the famous Maroons.

The Maroons were slaves who escaped from their Spanish masters in Jamaica in 1655. Originally, these people had been brought to the Caribbean islands from Africa because the Spanish colonists in this part of the New World needed workers in their sugar cane fields. Britain also had colonies in the Caribbean, and in the 1650s the British began to take over the Spanish colonies. When the British attacked Jamaica in 1655, the slaves of the Spaniards saw their chance to escape. They went up into the mountains, and from their mountain strongholds they managed to beat back both the Spanish and the British. They began to be called Maroons because in old Spanish that word means mountaintop.

After a time, the new British rulers of the island gave up trying to defeat the Maroons. Instead, they signed a peace treaty with them. The Maroons got legal right to the lands they already controlled, and the British got relief from an embarrassing situation. Even now, people who know anything about the history of slavery, especially in the West Indies, have great respect for the Maroons. These people managed not only to escape from slavery but to stay free, even though armies were sent to recapture them. When Katherine Dunham went among them, they were still a proud, free people living in the mountains and very suspicious of outsiders. Dr. Herskovits and a few others had visited them for brief periods, but no outsider had ever lived among them for any length of time before Katherine arrived.

By the time Katherine went to Maroon country, she was 26 years old. By the standards of the hard life the Maroons lived she was already middle-aged. Maroon women her age had given birth to many children already, and their bodies were tired and worn, not lithe and supple as hers was. She was worlds away from them in experience, too. Most of the people she was about to study had never even been down from the mountains, much less on a ship. Also, she might think of herself as somehow related to them because she was a Negro and so were they, but they could not see any relationship between themselves and her. The Maroons had intermarried in the nearly 300 years since their escape. As a result, they were dark-skinned. By contrast, there stood Katherine, whose ancestry was not just African but Madagascan, French-Canadian, and even American Indian. She might have been of medium skin color in the United States, but here she was considered white.

Katherine had barely gotten used to these ideas when she came smack up against the practical differences of culture that Dr. Herskovits had warned her about. She slept on a mattress of river rushes that was laid on the floor. The Maroon food was so highly seasoned that she got stomach aches. She soon found out that the kerosene lamp she made notes by at night was such a luxury that she started feeling guilty about using it. And for a while she found herself in the defensive position of having to explain so much about who she was and what she was doing and how her equipment worked that she began to wonder who was doing the field research—the Maroons or her.

After Katherine had been with the Maroons for a few days, she was overjoyed to be asked to attend a dance. She was so excited she could hardly wait. The invitation meant that she had behaved properly and was going to be let in on the tribe's ancient secrets, or so she thought. But when she arrived at the dance she was astonished and disappointed at what she saw. The women wore dresses and the men wore trousers. The one musician played a fiddle, and the dance was not much different from a plain old square dance. "For heaven's sake," thought Katherine, "I could have stayed in Chicago and seen this!"

But she did not give up. Dr. Herskovits had warned her

that she would not be accepted right away. She had an idea that the Maroons didn't just do square dances all the time. She watched and listened every day, and at night by her kerosene lamp she made notes about how the people dressed and behaved. She made friends among the Maroons and gradually she learned that they had many ancient dances and rites. But these were discouraged by their chief, who thought that the ancient customs got in the way of the progress of his people. Katherine learned, too, that most of the young people disapproved of the old dances. In feeling this way, they were no different from the young people of any culture, who think their parents' way of doing things is old-fashioned.

Although Katherine eventually got to see some of the old tribal dances, including a war dance that had come directly from Africa, she was disappointed in her visit to the Maroons. These people had been exposed to the outside world enough so that their culture was no longer the "pure" culture she wanted to find. She hoped she would have better luck in other parts of the West Indies.

In Martinique she was able to watch the war dance called Ag'Ya and other dances that had been done on the island as far back as anyone could remember. In Trinidad, she saw part of a Shango ceremony. Shango was the god of thunder and lightning worshiped by the Yoruba tribe in West Africa and brought to the New World by Yoruba slaves. A Shango priest allowed her to watch from the window of a hut while outside he performed the secret rites. The priest had a knife and a live white rooster, and he was clearly going to slit the rooster's throat. Katherine turned on her motion picture camera and began to record the event. But the priest heard the sound of the camera and came after her in a rage, waving the knife. A friend saved her, but the experience frightened Katherine. She decided not to try to take any more moving pictures.

At last, in Haiti, Katherine found what she had been looking for. Out in the "bush country," far away from the cities and towns, she found people whose belief in voodoo was as strong as it had been hundreds of years earlier.

The country now known as Haiti was discovered by Christopher Columbus in 1492 and was a Spanish possession until 1697 when Spain gave it up to France. Both the Spanish and the French imported African slaves to work the island's large sugar and coffee plantations, and because the plantations were so large and isolated from each other, the slaves were able to continue many of their African customs, including their religion. The majority of the slaves were of the Fon tribe from the Dahomey region of West Africa. Their religion, called *vodun* after the Fon word for god, came to be commonly known in the United States as voodoo.

It was this strong religious tradition that helped the slaves to unite and overthrow their French masters in 1804. The new nation, which the revolutionaries called Haiti, was governed for a long time after that by men who were actually *vodun* priests.

By the time Katherine arrived on the island, Haiti was much like other Caribbean countries, at least on the surface. Katherine saw that the Haitians were in some ways like blacks in the United States. The color bar was very strong: the lighter your skin, the higher your status in the social order. Katherine won immediate acceptance among the Haitian upper classes, but she was not interested in them. She traveled out to the country villages, where the people were dark-skinned, lived in grass huts and slept on rush floor mats. She made friends with people in these villages, people who were not even allowed to enter her hotel in the capital city of Port-au-Prince.

These country people lived and thought very much like their ancestors had 100 or more years earlier. As they came to know and trust Katherine, they told her more and more about their customs and their religious rites. She was invited to witness a ceremony in which an important priest who had died returned from the dead to name his successor. And finally she was allowed to take part in a ceremony of initiation into the ancient *vodun* cult. She eagerly accepted because, as she explains, "You can't know dances in Haiti without knowing the cult worship, because dance grows out of the demands of the gods. You hear a certain rhythm and without seeing what is being danced you know by the rhythm what the dance is and to what god it is being danced."

To prepare for the ceremony, Katherine had to gather offerings for the gods: things like eggs and herbs and powders, two live cocks, trade beads, sugar cookies and strawberry soda. She also had to buy a white dress and veil. On the appointed day, she traveled out to the bush country. After all the offerings she had brought were taken from her, she and the other initiates were told to take off their clothes. Then a special paste of eggs, cornmeal, herbs, feathers and blood was smeared into her hair and a bandanna was tied around her head. After that, she and the others were told to lie down on the floor of a special hut. For three days and nights they lay there, their bodies fitting against one another like spoons. Every little while a bell rang or hands clapped, and that meant they could turn over or go to the bathroom, or take the small amounts of sacred food that were brought to them. All the while outside, drums beat.

Lying on the floor, crammed against each other, forced to

go without food, the nine initiates, who ranged in age from seven to 70, were supposed to be ripe for possession by various voodoo gods. And during this time each was visited by the particular god that the full-fledged members of the cult had decided was the appropriate god for him or her. Actually, this "god" was one of the members dressed up in the costume of the god. One of the people lying on the floor of the hut was visited by Papa Guedé, the drunken god of death and ceremonies. A young girl was visited by the goddess Erzulie, who looked to Katherine a lot like the Virgin Mary. Katherine herself was visited by Damballa, the serpent god. When most of the others were visited by their gods, they rose to go with them because they felt as if the gods had possessed them. Katherine did not go with the serpent god who visited her because she did not feel possessed.

On the third day, the initiates got up and dressed in their white clothes in order to be "wedded" to their particular gods. There was a huge feast of celebration and dancing to the beat of the drums. Katherine was fascinated by the dancing. There was one dance in particular that excited her so much that at last she, too, felt possessed by the gods. The most important movements were made by the shoulders, which the dancers pushed out and then jerked back to the rhythm of the drumbeats. For a brief time Katherine forgot who she was and where she was. She was completely caught up in the dance and the beat of the drums. But then she saw a young boy bite into the neck of a live chicken and the spell went away. Katherine ran to the hut of a friend and threw up. After a good night's sleep she returned to her hotel in Port-au-Prince.

She saw the ritual through to the end. That meant leaving the cornmeal and egg and feather mixture in her hair for a week and returning to the countryside at the end of that time to have it removed in a ritual manner. She did not think she had been possessed by any gods, or blessed with any special new powers, but her bush country friends did. Before leaving Haiti she agreed to give a dance performance at a theater in Port-au-Prince. She would be the second act in the program, following a blonde French singer, and she arranged for a whole row of seats to be set aside for her bush country friends. Only one woman came, and she did not understand that Katherine was to be the second act. All she saw was the blonde French singer and she thought it was Katherine making use of her new magical powers to turn herself into someone else. Katherine could never persuade her friends out in the countryside that she had not transformed herself into a white singer for the evening.

Katherine loved Haiti. It was the most beautiful place she had ever seen. She had made many friends of all classes there, and she did not want to leave them. But in June 1936 the period of her Rosenwald study grant was up, and she had to return to the United States. She dreaded going back, in a way. She wasn't worried about making her reports so she could get her degree in anthropology. She had accomplished what she had set out to do. She had gathered material on the customs and ceremonies of people of African heritage. She had learned dances that seemed to her to link the dances of American Negroes with the dances of Africans. On the personal level, she had discovered her own proud heritage and gained an understanding of her African roots. But she was troubled. She was not sure she really wanted to go on in anthropology. Her experiences in the Caribbean had made her want to dance more than ever.

At the same time, she had learned that in order to dance the dances, or even interpret the dances, of the cultures she had visited, she would have to use every bit of her anthropological knowledge, and more.

* * *

You must know the entire complex, the musical instruments, the rhythms, the songs and what they're used for and how they're used, the language, and the interrelationships among all the elements in this immense cycle that goes with *a single* dance. So-called ethnic dancers today, who just passed through some place and picked up a couple of things, are not *real* ethnic dancers. From my own anthropological training, I've learned that you practically have to put yourself into the skin of a person if you're going to claim to know anything about him or her. If I learned anything from my trip, it was that I couldn't come into a culture as a lady anthropologist who knew dance and leave with any real knowledge of that culture's dances. It just wouldn't be the real thing. In fact, I'm still after the real thing.

Katherine's ocean voyage back to the United States was not nearly as comfortable as her first trip by boat. There had been a delay in the final monies due for the trip from the Rosenwald Fund, and she had not counted on such a delay. She had overspent her living allowance all along. Practically penniless, she had to take deck passage on a French ship, much larger than the Dutch ship on which she had sailed southward. Her "cabin" was a mattress under the stars, and even if she was sure what was proper to wear to dinner she could not use that knowledge because deck passengers were not allowed in the dining room. A year earlier, she would have been ashamed to sleep on deck on a mattress, but now it did not bother her in the least, for she had learned in her travels that people did not need feather beds to sleep in dignity.

# SIX

BACK IN CHICAGO, KATHERINE WAS REUNITED WITH HER HUS-band, but her long absence had only widened the gulf between them. He had made his own life while she was away. Her experiences had taken her far away from him in more ways than just miles. They shared a roof but not much else.

Katherine polished her reports of her field work, and in the summer of 1936 was awarded a bachelor's degree in anthropology. Urged on by Dr. Redfield and Dr. Hersko-vits, she then applied to the Rockefeller Foundation for a grant to finance further studies toward her master's degree. Although she knew in her heart that dance, not anthropol-ogy, was what she wanted to pursue, she had no idea how to follow her heart. At least with anthropology there were clearly defined academic steps to take. Meanwhile, she got back in touch with her dancing group, which had been kept together in her absence by Ludmila Speranzeva.

Soon, she was as busy as ever with her dancing, for the Young Men's Hebrew Association in New York City had somehow learned of the existence of her group and invited them to perform in a program titled "Negro Dance Evening" to be held in March 1937.

New York was then, as it is now, the dance capital of the United States, and Katherine and her dance group would have jumped at the chance to perform even in a subway station there. The group traveled for 15 hours straight in two rattletrap cars and spent the night sleeping on the floor and even in the bathtub of a Harlem apartment before driving 15 hours back to Chicago, but all the discomfort was worth it. The audience at the YMHA loved the program Katherine and her group presented. It ranged from classical ballet to Haitian dances she specially choreographed. Even a few newspaper critics attended the show and wrote positive reviews. It was enough to cause Katherine to lean even more heavily toward dance and away from anthropology.

But she was in a quandary. How could she give up her studies in anthropology after the Rosenwald Fund and now the Rockefeller Foundation had given her their support? How could she face Dr. Redfield and Dr. Herskovits? She got up enough courage to ask Dr. Herskovits if he thought she could ask the Rockefeller Foundation to give her a grant to go to Europe to study other types of dancing instead of doing further work in anthropology, but he didn't think that was a very good idea. She went ahead anyway and was turned down. Not wanting to lose the Rockefeller grant altogether, in June of 1937 she asked that her fellowship be suspended. She might take it up again in October. Then she applied for a Guggenheim fellowship to continue her dance studies.

She did not get the Guggenheim grant, but by the time she was turned down she had pretty much decided the course of her future. And her decision was not tied to grants received or grants refused. She did not want to teach anthropology. *She wanted to dance.*

But she still felt guilty. She finally decided to confront both of the professors who had helped her so much over the last couple of years. Dr. Redfield understood how she felt. Dr. Herskovits did not. Katherine would always regret not being able to live up to the hopes of these two scholars. But she would never regret her final choice.

By this time the Great Depression was so bad that the federal government was doing all sorts of things to put people back to work. President Franklin D. Roosevelt had started job programs of every description, including programs for artists. Many artists, writers, actors, dancers and playwrights would get their start through these unique programs. What was especially remarkable, back in the 1930s, was that the government gave as much support to black artists as they did to white ones. In the major black population centers there were Negro groups set up and funded as well as white groups. Katherine got a job as dance director of the Negro Federal Theatre Project in Chicago. The group was just getting under way, and so she had complete control over the choreography for the opening recital, to be called "Ballet Fèdre" (Federal Ballet).

Katherine choreographed a variety of dances for the recital. They would show the range of talent of Chicago dancers who were part of the project and appeal to a wide audience. But the number she worked hardest on, and the one closest to her heart, was "L'Ag'Ya," a folk ballet based on the dance she had seen in Martinique. The entire recital, which was presented at the Great Northern Theatre on January 27, 1938, was well received by both audience and critics, but the part of the program the critics raved about most was the "fiery folk ballet with choreography by Katherine Dunham."

Fanny Taylor Dunham with Albert, Jr.

Katherine Dunham as a child

Katherine and Albert, Jr.

*Katherine Dunham,
aged about seventeen*

With her young students, c. 1938

The Dunham Troupe, c. 1935

With some friends during her research days in Haiti, 1936

Katherine Dunham, c. 1949

In L'Ag'Ya pose, c. 1947

Members of the Dunham Dance Company arriving in Paris, 1948

With Maurice Chevalier, the French entertainer, c. 1949

With her husband, John Pratt

With her daughter,
Marie Christine, 1956

View from one of the porches
at Habitation Leclerc, c. 1958

Katherine's work with the Negro Federal Theatre Project in Chicago brought her into contact with John Pratt, a Canadian-born white man who had studied art at the University of Chicago. Hired by the Theatre Project to design sets and costumes, he worked closely with Katherine, and the two found that they shared the same ideas about their work. Katherine was 28 years old and married at the time, and John was 24 and single. They were also of different races. But they found that they had many other ideas in common besides their ideas on art.

By the late 1930s "the Negro" was no longer very much in vogue among white people in the wealthy and intellectual classes. The Depression had put an end to all that. During more prosperous days it had been fun for these white people to go to Harlem and other big-city black communities and watch the natives dance and hear the jazz they played. But as the Depression deepened, these big-city black communities became very disheartening places. The sidewalks were filled with long lines of people waiting to be fed at the free soup kitchens, with beggars and peddlers selling apples. All this was not exotic at all. Ordinary blacks had known all along that there was poverty and sadness in their communities. The whites had just not seen it. But blacks were hit harder than anyone else by the Depression and someone would have to be blind not to see the despair and hardship.

This did not mean that all blacks were forgotten by the larger society. Writers like Langston Hughes managed to keep on earning a living. So did bandleaders like Duke Ellington and singers like Lena Horne. The "Negro Renaissance" had shown even many whites who were neither intellectual nor wealthy that black people had something to offer, at least in the field of entertainment. So

Katherine Dunham was not being foolish to think that perhaps she and her dance company could make it in the United States. The reaction of critics and audiences to "L'Ag'Ya" showed her that whites were aware of and interested in the new and different type of dancing she had presented. After more than a decade of thinking that anything a black person did was exotic, they were now responding positively to the real thing.

So Katherine took the bold step of hiring a professional manager to book her group in any town or city where there was work to be had, and soon they were traveling throughout the state. They even got to perform in Joliet, where a proud Albert Dunham, Sr., had suggested that his daughter's dance group should present a program to benefit a local scholarship fund. Katherine loved to be able to return to her hometown in triumph, to show all her friends and neighbors that she had made good. The only thing that marred her happiness and that of her father and stepmother was remembering that Albert, Jr., had not been so lucky. The brilliant young man who had always seemed to have such a bright future ahead of him was still in St. Elizabeth's Hospital in Washington, unable to live in the outside world.

John Pratt joined Katherine's touring company as its stage and costume designer. As they traveled together throughout Illinois, the two drew close. Her marriage to Jordis McCoo had always been a strange, incomplete relationship. Although McCoo danced with the Dunham troupe until March 1938, after that time his name was no longer listed on the program. Perhaps his job in the post office kept him from traveling with the rest. Or perhaps by that time he did not want to.

Katherine and Jordis were divorced in late 1938 or early

1939. On July 10, 1939, Katherine and John Pratt were married in Tecade, Mexico. They realized that as an interracial couple they would encounter problems, but they did not intend to allow their lives to be ruled by other people. Besides, in their particular world—the world of dance—most people did not care about skin color. Talent and energy and determination were far more important, and Katherine and John had these in abundance. The fact that they were of different races was as unimportant as the fact that Katherine was five years older than her husband. What counted was that they cared about the same things and were determined to be successful not just in Illinois but in New York, the dance and theater capital of the country.

# SEVEN

IN THE FALL OF 1939 KATHERINE AND JOHN GOT THEIR CHANCE
to go to New York. Louis Schaeffer of the New York Labor
Stage had seen her group perform at the YMHA in New
York, and he wanted her to be dance director of a show
about the International Ladies Garment Workers Union
called *Pins and Needles.* Katherine accepted immediately.
This was her chance to stay in New York long enough to
find a theater and present the Dunham dancers to the
sophisticated New York audience.

Katherine and John moved into an apartment at 43 West
66th Street. With Schaeffer's help, Katherine found that the
Windsor Theatre, just off Broadway on West 48th Street,
was available on Sundays. She also found a rehearsal studio
on West 21st Street. She gathered together a group of dancers, two of whom she had met as a result of the YMHA
performance and some of whom came from Chicago, and
began to rehearse them for her off-Broadway debut. Meanwhile, John Pratt set to work on scenery and costumes. On
Sunday, February 18, 1940, *Tropics and Le Jazz Hot*
opened at the Windsor Theatre. It included elements from a

variety of cultures, including a Cuban rumba, a Mexican rumba and two Peruvian numbers as well as a number called "Island Songs." It also included a suite called "Le Jazz Hot" and a folk ballet called "Br'er Rabbit and de Tah Baby" that featured black American dancing. The next morning's newspapers were filled with rave reviews. John Martin of the New York *Times* wrote:

> Katherine Dunham and her dance group made their New York debut last night at the Windsor Theatre and provided thereby a revelation of how excellent the Negro dance can be as an independent medium when it is in the hands of somebody who knows what to do with it. As a composer in general she has imagination and taste and a fine sense of the theatre. Her music is excellent and her costumes are ingenious and distinctly attractive. As a dancer she is not only lovely to look at, but has style and authority.

The critic for the New York *Herald Tribune* said, "Katherine Dunham has proved herself the first pioneer of the Negro dance, and dance enthusiasts will await her future contributions with decided interest."

Katherine was almost surprised at the warm reception of her show. Urged on by the critics, audiences packed the Windsor Theatre each Sunday, and left the theater raving over the performance. "We ran at the Windsor for thirteen consecutive Sunday afternoons, which was quite unusual in those days," she recalls. Newspaper articles continued to credit her with being the first to present Negro dance as a serious art. The New York *Times* critic said that opening night at the Windsor Theatre "may very well become a historic occasion."

Overnight, the Dunham Dance Company was in demand all across the country, and in May the group set off for Hollywood, stopping en route to play a limited engagement in Chicago. Katherine remembers well the audition for that engagement—the first nightclub show she did in that city:

I was doing a Spanish number, and for some reason I felt that I should have a chignon [an elaborate hairdo]. I was a great fan of Argentinians and Argentinitas. At any rate, I got all dressed up and put a Spanish dance record on the victrola and started dancing. When the record stopped, I realized I'd lost the wig at some point. I didn't know when. I was really embarrassed, but I got the job.

Her most vivid memory of the trip was when she visited her parents and introduced them to her new husband. Her father would retire from the dry-cleaning business that year, she learned. He and her stepmother would be comfortably well-off. If it hadn't been for continued worry over Albert, Jr., Katherine's family relationships would have been very comfortable.

After a month of performing in California, the Dunham troupe returned to New York to begin rehearsals for their debut on Broadway in an all-Negro musical drama called *Cabin in the Sky*. The people behind the show had really wanted Katherine alone, but she insisted that she and her group be booked as a unit. She got her way, and the group's salary of almost $3,000 a week was a staggering sum to them.

In *Cabin*, Katherine would have her first speaking role. She was to play Georgia Brown, a tough and wicked woman, and she found the character a bit hard to identify with.

In one scene she was supposed to hit her co-star, singer Ethel Waters, over the head with a beer bottle. She just could not bring herself to do it, and she threatened to quit if she had to. The script was changed according to her wishes.

The production, staged by the famous choreographer George Balanchine, opened in November 1940, and both Katherine and her group got more rave reviews. All in all, 1940 was a banner year for them, and it was capped off for Katherine when she learned that she would be included in the 1940 edition of *Current Biography*. Or, perhaps the year was really made special by a letter she received from Dr. Herskovits in Chicago. In it he said, "I think you were very wise to concentrate on your dancing and while it may have been nice to have you here I feel you are taking by far the better course."

Katherine liked performing on Broadway, but she had no intention of forsaking the concert stage. It was her first love. Her reasons for going to Broadway were primarily economic: "I had a company going and there simply was not enough work," she explains. Whenever their *Cabin* schedule permitted, she and her group gave recitals to sold-out audiences at the YMHA and elsewhere. Nor did she have any intention of giving up completely her more scholarly activities. During her first year in New York, she sold two articles about Martinique to *Esquire* magazine (she used the pen name Kaye Dunn). She lectured to anthropology classes at Columbia University, and in January 1941 she took ten members of her troupe to Yale University in New Haven, Connecticut, to show the Anthropology Club of the Yale University Graduate School how to use primitive materials in the field of theater. She was such an energetic and many-faceted person. No wonder she became so well-known so quickly.

Cabin in the Sky closed on Broadway in March 1941, and then began a cross-country tour. Katherine and her group went with it. After the show closed in San Francisco, the Dunham dancers played West Coast nightclubs for a while, but it was not long before they were in Hollywood.

Quite a few all-black movie musicals were being filmed in Hollywood at that time, and most of the performers who had become stars during the "Negro Renaissance" were the stars of these films. Duke Ellington and his band, and Cab Calloway and his, appeared in these films, as did singers Lena Horne and Ethel Waters, and tap dancer Bill "Bojangles" Robinson. Katherine and her group made several such pictures in Hollywood, including the famous *Stormy Weather*. They also appeared in pictures set in exotic locales, including places where Katherine had never been.

I was called in to do choreography for a movie set in Tahiti called *Pardon My Sarong*. They'd thought of me, they said, because they'd heard I'd spent so much time in Tahiti. I needed the job, so I said, well, you tell me the story and I can give you the type of choreography you need. But of course they were thinking of Haiti. I didn't disillusion them at all. I went ahead and took it.

Katherine Dunham did not have a long career in Hollywood, although she probably could have. She was regarded as an expert, and that was something that Hollywood producers respected.

The ignorance in Hollywood was so vast. I remember I used to love to see the Tarzan movies, but I always felt there was something phony about the black Africans in them. Of course that was because the majority of them were from Central Avenue in Hollywood.

A few attempts at authenticity were made back then. *King Solomon's Mines*, a 1937 picture, actually showed the Watusi as they are. Dennis Roosevelt's expedition into Watusi country, and the films he made there, made an impact and did something to change Hollywood's concept of what black African dancing should be.

This helped Katherine Dunham to be more respected and sought out as an expert by the Hollywood moguls. While working in Hollywood, she was able to insist on authenticity. When she did *Green Mansions*, which was supposed to be set in the Amazon jungle, she had a map of the Amazon pinned on her wall and the area where the story was set pinpointed. "I had photographs of the Indians themselves and their ceremonies, and we worked as much through those materials as we did on the dance steps," she recalls.

Katherine Dunham wishes that there were more people in Hollywood now who went to the same amount of trouble. "Cetain things are still phony. You'll still find a movie with a tribe that eats fire even though it really isn't done in that particular tribe. And you'll still find actors who will do just what they are told to do, even though they know better, to get the job."

But in Hollywood, then as now, most people didn't care anyway. All they wanted was something colorful and exciting. They weren't concerned if it was real or not.

What they did care about was the racial makeup of the cast, and this is where Katherine Dunham ran into trouble in Hollywood. "It was the people in the company—the people the camera would show—that caused the problem," she says.

> When I was forming the company, from about 1938 on, the ideal black dancer was light-skinned, somebody who had danced at one of the famous whites-only nightclubs, like the Cotton Club. But that was not my ideal. My company was what you might call a "Third World Company" from the beginning. We had Cubans, West Indians, Latin Americans, and their complexion didn't matter. What mattered was their talent.

But in Hollywood, complexion counted more than talent. Movie producers wanted Katherine to cast light-skinned dancers in all roles. She refused to change the composition of her company. "I know that it cost me a career in Hollywood," she says.

The extreme color-consciousness in Hollywood naturally extended from the film set to the social atmosphere in the country's film capital. The movie-star world was much different from the world of theater and dance, and Katherine much preferred the latter. In the world of theater and dance people did not care about skin color or social class as much as they cared about talent. But in Hollywood there were strong class and color lines. Big-name stars only socialized with other big-name stars, and even minor white actors snubbed the well-known black actors. Next to the money, the only thing Katherine liked about Hollywood was the climate, and its closeness to the sea. She and John rented a large house on the ocean, and she often walked the beach to relax and think. During those walks she would think of Haiti and hoped she would one day be able to return there.

Her dream was to spend about half the year in Haiti, where she would buy a big house and open a dance school, and to spend the other half of the year on tour making the money needed to live and work in Haiti.

After about a year in Hollywood, Katherine decided it was time to get back to the concert stage. The money would not be as good, and the living would not be as easy as in Hollywood, but Katherine felt stifled. Besides, she was never really satisfied with her film choreography. "I never see the completed film," she explains. "I just see the rushes, and I've never yet been satisfied with what I've seen."

She needed more room for creativity, and she felt that her dancers did, too. So she signed up with impresario Sol Hurok, who booked the troupe for a tour that would take them throughout the northern part of the United States and Canada. For the next several months the group got to be creative. They also experienced the discomforts of traveling all the time and of coming up against racial prejudice almost constantly.

The group almost never performed below the Mason-Dixon Line—a line drawn across the map of the United States before the Civil War to separate the free states from the slave states. There was just too much racial prejudice in the South. But Katherine and her company learned first-hand how deep was the racial prejudice in parts of the North as well. Their show, *Tropical Revue*, might be booked into major theaters, but the group could not spend the night in major hotels. They were forced to search out hotels and boarding houses that would take them, and this was not just physically tiring, it also took a heavy toll on their hearts. Katherine was not one to take this kind of discrimination lying down. She filed and won legal suits against some of the big hotels that refused to accommodate her. She also spoke out against policies of segregated seating in the theaters where the group performed.

> Usually, as soon as I found out that the theater was segregated I would raise such a scandal about it—hold the curtain and do everything possible to make the management uncomfortable—that the management would give in. We ended up playing to only one segregated audience, and that was at the American Theatre in Louisville, Kentucky. I was really in a bind with Mr. Hurok and with the management [advance money had been paid the Dunham troupe]. But at the end of the show I did tell the audience what had happened and my feelings about it. I told them that unfortunately we would not return to appear before them until people such as we were could sit beside people such as they were. It was 1943, right in the midst of World War II, and I reminded the audience of that. What I said had an impact because the following week Marian Anderson appeared, and the theater was desegregated from then on.

By the summer of 1943, Katherine and her troupe were eager to get back to the more racially liberal city of New York. There, in September, the group opened *Tropical Revue* at the Martin Beck Theatre. It contained some of the most popular numbers from the 1940 revue, plus some new ones. Among the most popular of these was "Rites de Passage." It dealt with fertility and death rituals and was based directly on Katherine's anthropological field work in the West Indies. During the run of the revue Katherine added new numbers, including a piece by Aaron Copland written especially for her, and the revue was so popular that it was extended to six weeks, which, said New York *Tribune* critic Edwin Denby, "establishes it already as a unique success for an entire evening of dance entertainment."

In his review of the show, critic John Martin of the New York *Times* pointed out, "Miss Dunham herself is as always a charming entertainer, not interested in the least in starring herself. She has put together an excellent company of dancers, and has given them every opportunity to show their talents." Martin's statement was very perceptive. For a variety of reasons Katherine Dunham herself was becoming a less visible presence among the Katherine Dunham dancers.

One reason was age and physical condition. By the fall of 1943 Katherine was 34 years old, and for a dancer that is past prime. Also, she had developed arthritis. She thought perhaps it had come on as a result of lying on the floor of the Haitian hut for three days and nights, but whatever the source of the arthritis, it restricted her movements and prevented her from making the smooth movements her own choreography demanded. Her interest in choreography was another reason. Back in 1940 and 1941, she had assured interviewers that she was not a great dancer. Her footwork was unexceptional, she said. Where she really excelled was in choreography—in planning and directing dances and in training dancers to perform them. The writer of the article on Katherine that appeared in the 1940 *Current Biography* characterized her ability as "partly executive," and by the middle 1940s Katherine was being called on to use every executive ability she could muster.

World War II was in progress, and John Pratt had been drafted. Based at Fort Eustis, in Virginia, he expected soon to be sent overseas. That left Katherine to handle alone the managing of the costumes and sets and stage production on top of the choreography and training. But she rose to the occasion, and then some.

After playing in New York for a two-week stint that wound up being extended to three months, the company went on tour for a year with *Tropical Revue*, and it was a hard year for everyone. The group came up against the same discrimination on the part of hotels and restaurants and theaters as they had on the earlier tour. In some cities like Boston, they also came up against censorship and had to remove some of the more explicitly sexual dances from their program. These difficulties did nothing to relieve the usual pressures of a tour.

It is not easy for anyone to live out of a suitcase for long stretches of time, to eat restaurant and diner food, and to sleep in unfamiliar beds. There are always transportation delays because of bad weather and poor scheduling and problems working on unfamiliar stages. Katherine remembers how it was to work in theaters whose stages didn't have footlights: "In one number, my partner would throw me down on the floor and I would slide across it until I was stopped by the footlights. But in some theaters there weren't any footlights, and I'd wind up hanging into the orchestra. I usually managed to make it look as though it was intended to be that way."

The whole experience can get pretty tiring after a while. It is most exhausting for the director of the group. Katherine felt responsible for the dancers, who were all younger than she. For their own good, and for the good of the company, she did not want them to stay out late at night in a strange town, or to party until all hours. She wanted them to rest and eat properly and practice regularly. Many of the dancers resented her authority. For her part, Katherine likened a touring group to a bunch of children, with the difference being that children at least grow up and go out on their own.

Everyone was glad to return to New York in late 1944 to open at the Century Theatre with a new version of *Tropical Revue*. New York critics and audiences were glad to have them back, too. The show's run at the Century was a huge success. But Katherine's mind was only partly on *Tropical Revue* during that run. She was busy planning to start a new school.

Although Katherine's mixing of anthropology and dance had seemed and still seemed unusual to many people, she had become convinced that it was her work in anthropology that had led to her success as a dancer and choreographer. A dancer might have exceptional coordination, but if there was no understanding of the cultural elements that cause people to move the way they do, then the dancer would be nothing more than mediocre. Katherine wanted to have a school where students would not be taught just dance steps; they would be taught philosophy and sociology and anthropology and related subjects as well.

Katherine was not the first to come up with this idea. Back in 1920 in Los Angeles, dancers Ruth St. Denis and Ted Shawn had founded the Denishawn School. There they had taught philosophy and other arts as well as dance. Their most celebrated student had been Martha Graham. Katherine wanted to expand on the Denishawn School idea. She wanted to teach young dancers not just the dances but the customs and languages of other people so they could really live the dances. And she even went further than that. With the memory of the racial discrimination she and her troupe had suffered during their national tours fresh in her mind, Katherine Dunham wanted to teach young people that there were other ways of thinking and acting than just the ones they had grown up with. She saw her school as a place where students would learn racial tolerance and understanding above all. If they also learned to dance, so much the better, but a student could graduate with honors from her school even if he or she was not much of a dancer. All the student would have to have done well in was understanding the original purpose and effect of dance: to help people feel part of a larger community.

In late 1944 Katherine opened the Katherine Dunham School of Dance in the same studio in Caravan Hall that the famous dancer Isadora Duncan had once used. But the studio soon proved too small. Katherine did not have many students at first, but even the few she had found that they could not dance with wild abandon, for fear of smacking into a wall. Katherine started looking around for a townhouse where she and John could live and also operate the school, and in January 1945 the New York *Times* reported that she had bought a six-story private dwelling at 14 East 71st Street right next to the Frick Art Reference Library (now the Frick Museum) for these purposes. But this real estate transaction fell through, and Katherine still could not find a suitable space for her school. It was a great stroke of luck when later in 1945 Lee Shubert of the famous Shubert Theatre family offered her studio space rent free for three years. Katherine jumped at the offer and happily went about establishing her school on the top floor of an old Shubert theater at 220 West 43rd Street. It was a prime location, just west of Broadway, and this location helped make the school seem a serious one to prospective students and one that was somehow connected to the Great White Way. In just one week she had 12 new pupils.

The school grew quickly. Within a year, the Katherine Dunham School of Dance had 420 students and before long she would introduce all the subjects she felt they needed to learn, according to her own personal philosophy. By late 1946–early 1947 the school had been renamed the Katherine Dunham School of Dance and Theatre.

The student body was highly varied, and about one quarter was white. Nearly half of the pupils were children. The rest were young adults from the United States and from foreign countries like Ireland, Switzerland and Palestine as well as various French colonies. The French government had been impressed with Katherine's work in the French islands of the West Indies. In an effort to revive interest in native culture among its colonies, the government of France had decided to send promising young dancers from its colonies to the Dunham school.

In a way, the United States government was also sending students to Katherine. As World War II drew to a close, returning veterans began to arrive at her school. Under the GI Educational Bill of Rights they could attend at the expense of the government. Katherine accepted them, but she had to teach them tuition free for months before the government came through with the money.

Finally, Katherine had some paying students who wanted to become actors and who wanted to improve their body movement and stage presence. Two of them, Marlon Brando and Jennifer Jones, became stars.

The students were offered a well-rounded curriculum. Dance courses included ballet, modern dance, Dunham technique, tap and social dancing, and percussion. Courses directly associated with the theater included classical drama, speech, visual design, body movement for actors, theatrical production and staging, radio technique, and makeup. But early on, Katherine had introduced courses that one would not expect to be offered at a school of dance and theater: philosophy and anthropology and languages like French and Spanish and Russian. "The primary function of our school had to do with personal relationships," Katherine explained to a reporter for the New York *World-Telegram*, "but its expression happens to be through the theater." The courses on philosophy and aesthetics "were particularly useful to unite the thinking of students with varied backgrounds."

Katherine did not believe in diplomas. "I care a lot less about the idea of diplomas than the actual knowledge a person requires," she said. But in order to get the school approved for the GI Bill of Rights assistance she had to come up with at least a certificate system. So she established certificates for the completion of courses from one to five years.

Several members of the Dunham Dance troupe were teachers at the school. One of the most popular was a Haitian named Papa Henri Augustin. Katherine had met him during her first trip to New York, when she and her Chicago group had performed at the YMHA. Arriving in New York to stay, she had sought him out to be the drummer for her new group. He taught courses in percussion and in Creole songs. Katherine was very close to Papa Henri. He helped her with questions on Haitian folklore and was a sympathetic friend when the pressures of life seemed to bear down on Katherine.

She was as busy as a whole hive of bees. Besides running and teaching at her school, she was doing choreography on the side. In 1945 she choreographed dances for an all-black show called *Windy City*, and in the same year she not only choreographed the dances for, but acted in and co-directed another all-black show on Broadway called *Carib Song*. All the chorus dancers were from Katherine's troupe, and her co-star was the well-known dancer Avon Long.

Unfortunately the show was not successful. Although it was called a musical play of the West Indies, there was very little of a play about it. The plot line was so thin as to be almost nonexistent. Katherine played a farmer's wife who falls in love with a fisherman (Avon Long), but most of the show was taken up with Caribbean dances that had nothing much to do with the plot. The show soon closed, and Katherine went back to her teaching and on to other things.

In 1946 she was hard at work on a book about her experiences in Jamaica. Meanwhile, she and her company recorded cuts for a Decca album on West Indian music, did a one-hour special for television, and played nightclub engagements in New York and elsewhere. Most of these nightclub shows were made up of pieces from the earlier *Tropical Revue*, but Katherine was constantly coming up with new dances to keep her programs—and her dancers— fresh. She choreographed a new version of "L'Ag'Ya" for the 1946 show in New York that received rave reviews.

By the fall of 1946 Katherine's school had grown and diversified so much that she decided a new name and a new structure were in order. She also wanted it to be chartered by the State of New York in the hope of attracting more students (the charter would be granted in 1947). The overall institution would now be called the Katherine Dunham School of Arts and Research. Within it were three separate schools: the Dunham School of Dance and Theatre, the Department of Cultural Studies, and the Institute for Caribbean Research. The institution now offered two-, three-, and five-year courses leading to professional, teaching and research certificates, and the faculty comprised 30 teachers. It was operating under huge deficits, however. As a requirement for a charter, the State of New York insisted on a board of directors for the school, and by mid–1947 it would have such a board. Katherine felt a certain amount of relief to have some of the pressure taken from her shoulders.

For all of her executive talents, Katherine never really saw her school as a money-making business. It was rather a labor of love. She was more concerned that her students learn how to get along in the world than that they become famous. She let many pupils attend classes who could not afford to pay tuition. The tuition fees the school did receive were not enough to pay for equipment and teacher's salaries. Meanwhile, the school was still staying rent-free in the loft of the Shubert theater.

EIGHT

IN 1946 JOHN PRATT WAS DISCHARGED FROM THE ARMY AND rejoined his wife in New York. He arrived just in time to share her woes about all the debts she owed on the school and her excitement about a new show that she was sure would be a big success and help pay off some of those debts. John would do the costumes and sets.

The show was called the *Bal Nègre*, and it opened at the Belasco Theatre on Broadway in November 1946. Like earlier Dunham shows, *Bal Nègre* was a mixture of old and new numbers, and it attempted to cover a range of black dance and culture styles. "L'Ag'Ya," combining the Martinique wrestling bout with origins going back to Africa and a voodoo hypnosis ritual called "Majumba," was included in the program. So was a Shango scene that Katherine had originally choreographed for *Carib Song*. One of the most popular pieces was "Haitian Roadside," which combined bits of Haitian folklore in a way that was both lively and convincing. There were short rumbas and other pieces from Spanish Caribbean culture, and a section on American rag-time. The show was a great success. Originally scheduled for a four-week run, it was extended several more. Happily, Katherine put her profits into the school and made plans for yet another tour.

This time, the tour began in Mexico. In the middle of April 1947, the Dunham dancers arrived in Mexico City for a four-week stint at the Esperanza Iris theater. Unfortunately, their baggage did not arrive with them. All their costumes and scenery were still in transit, and they were scheduled to open that very night. Like real troupers, they went on anyway, in their rehearsal clothes and without scenery or props. The sold-out audience loved them.

In Mexico, Katherine and her troupe experienced red-carpet treatment for the first time. Invitations poured in from diplomats and other officials, and from the leading artists, intellectuals and society people. Katherine was invited to meet the president of Mexico, Miguel Alemán Valdés. She was also invited to give a lecture in anthropology at the Palacio de Bellas Artes. The press followed her daily activities as if she were a queen. Because her name was hard to pronounce, she became known as "La Katerina," and every day the newspapers carried stories about "La Katerina" and her group. She was such a smash that she had to cancel the group's reservations in Acapulco again and again. At last the troupe left Mexico City and went on to other areas of the country, even to the Yucatán Peninsula. Then they toured the United States. *And then they went to Europe.*

Actually, the troupe returned to New York for a time before boarding a ship to England. Everyone had things to attend to at home, and Katherine had much to do before she could leave. Most important, she had to see to her school. Attendance had fallen off in her absence, and the school was as deeply in debt as ever, despite the fact that it now had a state charter and a board of directors. Since she wanted it to be able to go on without her, she had to turn over most of the profits from the recent North American tour to its business manager. She and John also had to choose some new dancers for the tour from the students at the school. Among these new recruits was a young woman named Eartha Kitt, who had taken advantage of the variety of courses offered at the school. She had taken language courses and courses in body movement because she realized that "a pretty face isn't everything." When Katherine and John's affairs in New York were as settled as they could make them, they and the troupe set off to conquer Europe.

Perhaps "conquer" is a poor word to use when talking about Europe in 1948, since it had been resisting conquest by the Germans for several years. The Dunham troupe would see some beautiful scenery and awesome historic sites there, but they would also see areas that had been reduced to rubble by German bombs and long lists of soldiers who had died defending their countries. Of course American families had lost fathers and husbands and sons in the war, too, and they had been forced to endure rationing of some foods. But bombs were never dropped on the United States, and compared to some of the European countries, America had been hardly touched at all by the war.

Still, Europe had survived, and after the long years of war the people of England and France and Italy and elsewhere were eager to laugh and have fun again. In nearly every country they visited, the Dunham troupe was welcomed with open arms.

They opened with *Caribbean Rhapsody* at London's Prince of Wales Theatre on June 2, 1948, and were so successful that two months later they were still in London. The British had some awareness of Negro culture because of their colonies in the West Indies and elsewhere, but most of the colored colonials who traveled to England or lived there had attended British schools and were as properly British as the white natives of the British Isles. Thus, Katherine and her dancers were an exciting new experience to the English.

She told a reporter for the New York *Herald Tribune*:

In our concert, at the end of the first act, we [would] dance a number called "Shango"—full of the deep drumbeats of tom-toms. The drumbeats always made the English trumpet players in the orchestra break down and cry—and when the curtain would go up the audience was always dotted with men and women who had fainted! That never happened in any country except inhibited, conservative England. . . . I am sure the English people haven't had enough butter and eggs these last ten years. That fainting must have been a symptom of some form of malnutrition.

Every critic in London acclaimed them. The critic of the *Daily Express* called the show "the fastest and most colourful show that London has seen for many years." Critics who usually had little use for modern dance had considerable praise for Dunham dancing. One said that Katherine's barefooted company made classical dancers seem like waxwork figures. Another wrote, "For the average spectator, perhaps, the high 'entertainment value' of her work may obscure its more solid qualities and keen intelligence, knowledge and artistry behind it. But the unity and beauty of her stage ensembles make some of our own ballet productions look more than a little primitive."

While in London, Katherine was invited to give a lecture to the Royal Anthropological Society. Her topic was "The

Occurrence of Cults Among 'Deprived' Peoples." She was also made an honorary member of the society.

After London, the Dunham troupe toured other British cities. In Manchester, Katherine experienced one of the hazards that were a natural result of her insistence on exciting, exuberant stage shows. In the number "Vera Cruz," a Mexican piece, Katherine would come onstage in a dress with an 18-foot-long train. She would meet her lover, and when they heard someone coming both would hop into a hammock that was stretched from one side of the stage to the other. With her lover hidden under her train, Katherine would pretend to read a book, but eventually the lover would get tired of suffocating under the train and would jump out.

John Pratt recalls, "This was a very tough moment in terms of staging. When the lover jumped out, the hammock would turn over—unless the stage hands held on to it to equalize the weight."

Every now and then, something would go wrong. Once, when the lover jumped out, the whole hammock fell down. "I fell with it," Katherine remembers. "But we had to go on as if nothing had happened. I wonder what the audience thought."

In Manchester, England, the hammock completely turned over, and Katherine and her lover spilled out onto the floor. "The prop man insisted on using round rings," John Pratt recalls. "I knew they wouldn't be stable enough."

Although Katherine and her troupe were well received and well treated in England, the staid British were hardly the hosts that the Mexicans had been. But in Paris, where the Dunham troupe went next, that feeling of royalty came to them all over again. In Paris, they were not just entertainers, they were *artistes*.

Although the troupe arrived in Paris a week before their opening night, their luggage did not, just as in Mexico. After a couple of days, Katherine began to get desperate, so she wired her London representative and asked him to trace the baggage. The London agent located the luggage at the port of Cherbourg. The dock workers had gone on strike, French troops had been sent in to make the strikers go back to work, and the two sides were fighting in the streets. The dock workers had used the Dunham troupe's baggage to make a road block! Katherine would recall:

For four days our representative pleaded with the police to rescue our trunks—didn't work. Then, a local impresario collared our man and the leader of the stevedores, who finally asked: "To whom does the baggage belong, please to repeat?"

"To Katherine Dunham, the famous American dancer—she opens tomorrow night in Paris—her scenery and clothes are in the trunks you use for the blockade."

"Ahhh—I did not know. Katherine Dunham, the *artiste*! Why did not someone tell me? In France, the arts are the most important thing! Certainly more important than our little war. Hurry, we shall ship your trunks to Paris *immédiatement!*"

Anyone who was anybody in Paris invited Katherine and others in her troupe to dinner, to parties, to receptions in their honor. Other people fell over each other to make the first invitations to fill whatever remaining hours the dancers might have available. Newspaper photographers and reporters recorded their every public movement. Katherine and John, who fell in love with Paris and wanted to walk every inch of it, began to feel a little bit resentful over all the attention. "It is nice to be liked," Katherine remarked, "but in Paris the people devour you!" To escape some of the pressures of celebrity, Katherine and John moved to a hotel on the outskirts of Paris. There, they could shop daily at the open-air markets and eat at the small family restaurants without being recognized. Katherine took up painting at this time, because she wanted to have a lasting record of the French scenery she loved so much.

Katherine decided that she painted very well, and so one month after she started painting she held an exhibition of her work. If others thought she was rushing things a bit, she did not agree. She had great confidence in herself when it came to anything creative. She had published articles and was a successful dancer and choreographer, so why couldn't she also be a successful artist?

What did critics think of her paintings? "They were honestly *bewildered*," Katherine later reported in triumph. In Milan, where she exhibited, too, one critic said her paintings looked like "globs of strawberry jam." Two years later, a reporter in New York looked at photographs of her paintings and said they looked just as good upside down. "That," said Katherine with a grin and a wink, "is one of the tests of *true* art!"

The young dancers in Katherine's troupe thrived in the appreciative atmosphere of Paris. The young American blacks found in Paris an absence of racism and a feeling of belonging that they had previously experienced only in Mexico City—and Paris was so much more romantic. There were no segregated hotels or restaurants, no theaters where blacks could sit only in the balcony. In Paris, a black man and a white woman could walk down the street, and no one would even turn a head to look. There was a freedom that these young dancers had never felt in their native land, even if it was supposed to be "the land of the free." A number of the Dunham dancers chose to stay in Paris because of the feeling of freedom there. One of them was Eartha Kitt. She left the troupe to become a successful nightclub singer both in Europe and in the United States. Other members of the troupe who left at that time were Talley Beatty, who had been with Katherine since Chicago and danced in the original New York YMHA performances, Bobby Capo, and Jean-Leon Destine, both talented and seasoned performers.

Every time someone left the troupe, Katherine sent back to her school for a replacement. But the new dancers were not always as talented as they should be. Despite its financial difficulties, the Dunham School in New York was by now well-known, and other dance companies were sending representatives to hire away the best students. Katherine could not prevent these companies from "stealing" talented students who had paid full tuition all along, but she did feel that the students on scholarship owed her something. She directed the school authorities to have the scholarship students sign agreements giving the Dunham Dance Company the first chance to hire them.

Even some of those members of the company who remained proved hard to handle in Paris. They stayed out too late and lived too lavishly and didn't like it one bit when Katherine started fining them for being late or missing practice. And if all this was not hard enough to handle, Katherine was struck at this time by a loss that she would forever after refer to as the great tragedy of her life. In May 1949, Albert, Jr., died at St. Elizabeth's Hospital in Washington, D.C.

Albert's death was all the more tragic because he was almost ready to leave the hospital when he died. At last his mental disease had been cured, or at least brought under control, and he was looking forward to taking up his life of teaching and learning again. Then, he was struck down by a physical disease—tuberculosis. Katherine learned that his death had been inevitable for a long time, for by the time he had won his fellowship at the University of Chicago he had contracted tuberculosis and his condition worsened as time went on. Katherine would always wonder if Albert had got tuberculosis from cleaning their father's old dust wheel, but there was no point in blaming her father at this late date. She knew that her father mourned Albert, Jr.'s, death, too. She made a brief trip back to the United States to be with her family, but she could not leave her troupe alone in Europe for long.

After Paris, the Dunham Dance Company toured other parts of France, the Netherlands, Italy, Germany and some of the Scandinavian countries. Sometimes there was a week or more between bookings, and Katherine had to pay for her troupe's lodging and meals even though there was no money coming in. There were also special taxes and fees to be paid and problems with taking money from one country to another. And then, there were problems with the attitudes of people in other parts of Europe.

The audiences and critics in the other countries were somewhat taken aback by the Dunham shows. Their staid formality and sense of proper behavior were, in turn, a bit hard for Katherine and her troupe to understand. In Amsterdam every performance was sold out and the audience was completely awed—so awed, in fact, that they didn't recover in time to applaud very much after the show was over. The only dancing of colored peoples the Dutch had previously experienced was the restrained Indonesian style. They were not prepared for the exuberant and sen-

sual Dunham dancing—nor for Katherine's own exuber-
ance. As an American reporter in Paris wrote, "The impresario, Bob Peters, came out to make a typically Dutch
formal little speech of appreciation, whereupon Miss Dunham kissed his bald head, completely upsetting his equilib-
rium."

In Stockholm, Sweden, Katherine was not told in
advance that the King and his party would be attending the
troupe's first performance. Katherine came out on stage
with a bird cage on her head and props in each hand, and
did a double take when she saw that the Royal Box was
occupied. She gave a little extra to her performance but
wished she had been warned so she could have planned
something special. Later, her local agent told her she should
have bowed to the King, even if she did have a bird cage on
her head!

Also in Stockholm, some people complained that some
numbers in the show were too sexual. Katherine and her
group were surprised at this reaction from the supposedly
liberal Swedes.

Katherine was relieved to receive an invitation to go to
the 1949 Bicentenary Exposition in Haiti. She left her
troupe and all its problems and traveled to the island she
had fallen in love with years earlier. There, she was treated
like royalty and awarded the Haitian Legion of Honor
medal. In many ways, she felt as if she had come home, and
when she rejoined her troupe in Europe she told her husband that she would very much like to buy property
there.

The European tour ended in August, and none too soon,
in Katherine's opinion. Everyone was exhausted and ill-
tempered. Katherine had found herself drinking even in the
middle of a show. The tour had been highly successful, but

the troupe hardly felt triumphant. They just felt like going home.

Arriving back in New York in the fall of 1949, the Dunham company rested for a few weeks and Katherine saw to the business of her school. Then word came that her father had died, and she made a trip to Joliet. It was hard losing both her father and her brother in the same year, but she took her brother's death harder. It seemed to her terribly unfair that such a brilliant life and career had been interrupted, and she determined to make a mark on the world that would be big enough for both her and Albert.

NINE

BY APRIL 1950 THE DUNHAM DANCE COMPANY WAS BACK ON
Broadway with a new show, *Caribbean Rhapsody*, at the
Broadway Theatre. Critics saw a new style in the show and
decided that it was because of the European tour. "Playing
in Europe has apparently given the company a sense of
being exotic, which it could never have acquired here,"
wrote John Martin in the New York *Times*. Some critics
praised the new sophistication of the dancers' style. Others
mourned the absence of the abandon and driving force of
the earlier years. Katherine wondered if there was any
truth in these pronouncements. "When I came back to New
York from the West Coast, they said I had 'gone Hollywood.' When I went back to the Coast, they said I had 'gone
Broadway.' Maybe I do change with my locale." Whether
or not their dancing style had changed, the company, which
included Talley Beatty again (he had changed his mind
about staying in Paris), had indeed got used to feeling special, and so the old racial slights they sometimes received on
the streets of New York seemed even more painful than

they had before. Soon, they were looking forward to their Latin American tour, which was to begin shortly after their run ended at the Broadway Theatre.

But in Latin America they came up against racism, too, and that seemed startling to find in a country like Brazil, where the majority of the population was brown-skinned. In São Paulo the company was refused admittance to a major hotel. Katherine brought suit against the hotel management just as she had at American hotels in the Middle West years before. The suit resulted in the passage of an anti-discrimination law in Brazil. There were no unpleasant incidents in Argentina, where the company was constantly wined and dined by President Juan Perón and his wife Eva.

At the end of the Latin American tour, the company toured Jamaica, and there Katherine found two Haitian friends. One had moved to Jamaica because of a job, but the other had been forced to leave Haiti. President Dumarsais Estimé, who had befriended Katherine during her anthropological study trip to Haiti years before and who had invited her back for the 1949 Bicentenary Exposition, had been overthrown by a Haitian army coup. He was living in exile in Jamaica, hoping from there to gather enough support among ordinary Haitians to enable him to regain office. The things he told Katherine about what was going on in Haiti worried her. Only recently she and John had leased an old villa in Haiti and were planning to take the whole company there for six months of rest and relaxation after the tour. As it turned out, the main problems Katherine had in Haiti came from her own company and her own family.

The villa was called Habitation Leclerc, and it was once the home of Pauline Bonaparte Leclerc, the sister of French emperor Napoleon Bonaparte. It was a crumbling old place and was said to be haunted, but it had lovely grounds and several pools. Katherine had fallen in love with it the first time she had seen it. It was also big enough to accommodate her whole company. Twenty-four people arrived with her at Habitation Leclerc, including 15 dancers, musicians, composers, business managers and secretaries.

The new president of Haiti, Paul Magloire, welcomed the whole troupe and did not appear to hold Katherine's friendship with former President Estimé against her. It seemed to Katherine that every time she turned around she was being invited to some dinner or reception, or being asked to put on a special performance for the president. So there were no political problems.

What marred the peace of Habitation Leclerc was the boredom of the company. They grew tired of lying around the pools. Katherine urged them to journey out to the country villages and see the native rituals and dances firsthand, as she had. But they were not interested. They were more interested in going to the few bars and nightspots in the nearby towns. In Katherine's opinion, the members of the troupe missed being celebrities. Except for the president and his wife, the people of Haiti were not all that impressed with the Dunham dancers, and the Dunham dancers seemed to feel the need to impress.

Katherine's stepmother did not much like life at Habitation Leclerc either. Shortly after their arrival, Katherine had sent for Annette, expecting the older woman to be as enchanted with the beautiful countryside as she was. But Annette did not approve of the informality of life there. She missed her church meetings and her television programs back home. Sadly, Katherine and John admitted to themselves that some of their dreams for Habitation Leclerc would not work, especially the one about making the estate a permanent home for the Dunham company. But they decided to buy it and fix it up anyway, for their own use and for their retirement.

At the end of six months, the Dunham dancers went on the road again. After playing at a few western U.S. nightclubs, they set off on their second European tour. This was as successful as the first had been, but it was also just as tiring and nerve-frazzling. By now Katherine was wondering if she had the strength to continue such a life.

She longed to settle down. She was 43 years old now, and she did not have the physical strength she'd had in her younger days. Her arthritis had gotten worse over the years, and it was getting harder and harder to keep up with her young company. Also, she was beginning to feel that she had missed something by not having a family. John Pratt felt the same way, and in 1952, although their life was still unsettled, they adopted a five-year-old Martinique child of mixed parentage named Marie Christine Columbier. The little girl traveled with the troupe for a while, and seeing a child in the midst of all the craziness of a touring group caused Katherine to feel even more like giving up the whole thing.

She began to wish she could devote her full time to her school. She had always enjoyed teaching, and it seemed like such a sane life compared to the life she was leading. But she could not afford to stop performing. She was too deeply in debt. The school was still not paying for itself—not by a long shot—and of course there was the mortgage on Habitation Leclerc and all the needed improvements that required money. There was just no way she could stop touring. Then, just at the time when she was longing most fervently to devote a lot of personal attention to her school, she was advised to close it.

The school was so deeply in debt that it was affecting the

morale of both students and teachers. It was costing Katherine $800 a week just to keep it open, and this financial burden was affecting her morale, too. Katherine wanted desperately to continue the school. She argued with her advisers that she needed it: she needed to be able to recruit its students for her company, she needed the space for her company's rehearsals when they were in New York. But eventually she gave in. The school was too much of a financial drain. The money she kept plowing into it could be put to better use. And so in 1954 the school that had given a start to a whole generation of young black dancers and also taught a thing or two to young white actors like Marlon Brando and Jennifer Jones closed after ten years.

Katherine felt sick about having to close her school. To get her mind off it, she began making plans to put up a small tourist hotel on the grounds of Habitation Leclerc. But she still had so many debts that she couldn't find anyone who would lend her money to build the hotel. There seemed nothing for her to do but to continue touring, which was getting harder on her physically and emotionally with every passing year.

She had operations on both knees to remove cartilage that had built up from her years of dancing. But there was no operation for arthritis, nor any known cure. She had to suffer that pain with no hope of relief. Naturally, her physical condition affected her dancing, but she managed almost to turn her disabilities into an advantage. She learned to make the most of the subtle movement, the single expressive gesture. When the troupe returned to New York in the fall of 1955 after almost five years away, critics noticed and praised the change in her style.

Wrote Walter Terry of the New York *Herald Tribune,* "In her new revue at the Broadway Theatre, Miss Dunham continues to exert her quite irresistible charm without exerting herself muscularly." And John Martin of the New York *Times* noticed how she artfully contrasted her effortless style with the wild energy of her young dance troupe:

> She is the complete mistress of the art of underplaying. She sings without raising her voice, she dances with a minimum of technical expenditure, she invites all kinds of equatorial states of mind by the merest twitching of a hip or rippling of a shoulder. . . . As if to set off this very coolness . . . she has a large and energetic company in almost constant energetic motion about her, and the more vigorous they are, the more enchantingly in a realm apart she seems.

Katherine Dunham was 46 years old by the fall of 1955, but in spite of her arthritis and knee operations she was not a has-been trying to hold on to former glory. She had simply refined her style to fit the realities of her physical condition. In a way, she had done the same thing with her dances. Years and years after certain numbers had first been introduced they were still being presented by the Dunham dancers, and often these were the numbers that were most highly praised for their artistry. A dance like "L'Ag'Ya" was 20 years old by now, but it had been refined and added to and was as exciting in the 1950s as it had been in the 1930s. As critic John Hawkins of the New York *World Telegram and Sun* wrote, "because she continually edits and builds, the most familiar items on her program often seem the most exciting." There was always something new, but Katherine never sought newness for its own sake. She understood that true art was lasting, that just as people will go to see and dancers will want to dance a ballet like *Swan Lake* year after year, it was possible to create a folk ballet with lasting power. Her programs were always a blend of old numbers and new, West Indian dances and black American ones, but she never lost sight of her art. And that, combined with her drive, is what kept her and her company from being a short-lived fad.

When Katherine had arrived in New York and opened on Broadway in 1940, she and her dance style had been something of a curiosity. The fact that she had a degree in anthropology and had done field work in the West Indies was almost as interesting to critics as her dancing. In fact, if it hadn't been for her academic credentials, she might not have received nearly as much attention as she did get. But she and her company would have fallen from the spotlight very quickly if she had not managed to present programs that were both entertaining and serious in their art. By 1955 she and her company were practically an American institution—at least as close to being an institution as a group of Negro dancers could be in America at that time. They were also well-known in Europe, and by 1956 they were going to parts of the world that were not on the ordinary tour of most American entertainers—places like Australia and New Zealand and the Far East.

TEN

THE AUSTRALIA-ORIENT TOUR WAS TO BE AN AMBITIOUS BUT risky one. There were no advance fees for the company, and transporting all the dancers and secretaries and prop people, not to mention the costumes and props themselves, required monies Katherine did not have. So, she sold a diamond necklace to pay for the trip to Australia and counted on the fees earned there to pay for the troupe's further travel to the Orient.

John Pratt went along on the tour, but their daughter, Marie Christine, did not. She went to Joliet to stay with Annette Dunham and attend school there. It was just as well that she did not accompany her parents on the tour, for it was not a happy one. During it, John Pratt would leave the group and return to Haiti, and at its end Katherine would disband the Dunham Dance Company.

Several things contributed to the problems on the tour. As always, the major one was money. Katherine worried about money constantly, and she had good reason to do so. The costs of lodging and feeding and transporting so many people were staggering. Worrying about money all the time put Katherine in a bad mood. And the group's reception in Australia did nothing to improve her disposition.

There was obvious racism in Australia, a country where descendants of British settlers looked down their noses at the native aborigines. It showed up in the reviews of the Dunham show when critics remarked that they could not see her in the darkness of the theater (because she was dark-skinned to their eyes). But some of the negative things the critics said about Katherine had nothing to do with either her color or her show. They had to do, instead, with Katherine's manner.

Katherine had long behaved in a regal way—like a queen who is always holding court. Everyone called her Miss Dunham, even her husband (she called him Mr. P.). She tended to keep people waiting, to change her mind a lot and expect everyone to do her bidding, and generally to have a very high opinion of herself—and these qualities had helped her to become as successful as she was. But during this tour, she became a complete tyrant. She would yell at her stage manager not to bother her and then later yell at him for not telling her what he'd been trying to tell her in the first place. She would give her secretary an order, change her mind and give another, then change her mind again and get mad at the poor woman for not being able to follow her wishes quickly enough. She demanded that her dressing room in each theater be specially decorated in Japanese style, and she wouldn't let anyone in with shoes on. Pretty soon she was sleeping in her dressing room instead of in the hotel room with her husband, because the two of them were not getting along.

John Pratt was a quiet, mild-mannered man who seemed to complement the moody, high-strung Katherine. But he was no weakling, and when his wife became more and more demanding and unreasonable he decided he'd had enough.

In the late fall of 1956 he left the tour and went to Haiti. That left Katherine alone, with no one to turn to. It also left her in charge of production, a responsibility her husband had held. As a result, she became even more ill-tempered. But she was determined to finish the tour. From Australia and New Zealand the group went to Singapore and Hong Kong and the Philippines, where new problems awaited them. Their shows were well received, but living conditions were almost unbearable. The intense heat bothered everyone, and Katherine spent what seemed like half her time trying to get fans and water coolers and food that did not make her dancers sick. Meanwhile, she learned that her stepmother was gravely ill, and she felt guilty for not being able to leave the tour and return to Joliet.

Because of Annette Dunham's illness, John arranged for Marie Christine to stay with relatives of his in Chicago while he found a suitable school for her in Haiti. Katherine approved of this. She missed her husband and·daughter and was pleased that they would soon be together. She wanted very much to leave the tour and all of its problems behind and join her family at her beloved Habitation Leclerc. By the time the tour reached Japan in the summer of 1957, she didn't care where she was as long as she did not have to be responsible for the Dunham dancers.

She was tired of traveling, tired of trying to come up with new ideas to keep her shows lively and her dancers interested, tired of being responsible for so many other people. She felt as if, in keeping track of everyone else for so many years, she had lost track of herself. She just did not have the energy to do it anymore. And she was also aware that she no longer had the disposition for it. She knew quite well that she had grown ill-tempered and unreasonable, but she couldn't seem to stop being that way. What she needed, she decided, was some peace, some time to rest and find herself. In early October 1957, the Australia-Orient tour ended, and so, at least for a time, did the 20-year-old institution called the Dunham Dance Company. It wouldn't be forever, she told the troupe. When they'd all had a good long rest from each other they would unite again. In the meantime, she would do all she could to see that they got jobs with other companies. Everyone parted as friends, because in spite of all the hardships of being on the road, in spite of all the bickering and bad feelings, the members of the group felt a strong bond, for they had been through a lot together and had shared the common dream of bringing their particular style of dancing to people all over the world.

ELEVEN

TWO WEEKS LATER, ANNETTE POINDEXTER DUNHAM DIED, and with her went Katherine's last link to her childhood. The event seemed to fit in with the way she was feeling, for she was feeling very much alone. There she was in Japan, thousands of miles away from anyone who loved or cared about her. She could have packed up and gone home to Habitation Leclerc. By this time, she and John had put aside the problems in their relationship that had caused him to leave the tour almost a year earlier. She missed him and she missed Marie Christine. But Katherine decided not to go home just yet. In Haiti, she would have to be a wife and a mother again, and she didn't want to resume those roles so soon after she had finally given up her role as head of the Dunham Dance Company. For a while she didn't want to have any role at all. She was 48 years old, and she wanted to have a little time without any responsibilities. She didn't want to be Miss Dunham or even Mother. She just wanted to be Katherine, and she wanted to find out who Katherine had been and had become.

She rented a large attic room with a terrace above a tailoring shop in Tokyo and furnished it with props left over when her company had disbanded. There, when the weather was good, she sat on the terrace and looked at Mount Fuji and tried to figure out her life. She was still not free from all cares. She had financial problems that were not solved by the disbanding of the company. There was Habitation Leclerc to worry about. John was doing much of the work on improving the property himself, but the monthly mortgage payments still had to be met, and she owed debts she had taken on to keep the company going. Also, she owed a considerable amount of money in back income taxes to the U.S. government. Her stepmother's death and the disbanding of the company and her own feelings about herself had caused Katherine to think a lot about her past. She started writing down her thoughts, and before long she had decided to write a book about her experiences. That would solve everything, she decided, because even in a sad and reflective mood Katherine Dunham had supreme confidence in herself. Naturally, she would write not just any old book, but a bestseller!

She soon found out that her idea of a bestseller was not the same as that of many editors. The editors to whom her agent in New York submitted her finished chapters kept urging her to write about the more glamorous events of her life and the important people she had known. Katherine intended to get to these things, but later. For the time being she wanted to concentrate on her early life and in her opinion her first 18 years were a book in themselves.

Her refusal to write the kind of book the editors wanted put her in a worse financial position. Without a contract and a sizable advance, she could not remain in Japan. She had to do something that would bring in money. Thus, she accepted an offer to choreograph the dance scenes in the Hollywood film *Green Mansions*.

In "Death," from "Rites de Passage," Paris, 1951

With her husband and the troupe, aboard ship in South America, c. 1955

In Paris, 1960

With M. Leopold Sedar Senghor, President of Senegal (second from left) in the presidential palace, Senegal, c. 1965. Also in photograph: Maurice Sonar Senghor (on extreme left), Katherine Dunham and John Pratt

With Thomas Gomez in the East St. Louis Office, c. 1969

With Senator Adlai E. Stevenson in his Washington office, together with some East St. Louis participants in the White House Conference on Children, 1970

Participating in an Arts Conference in East St. Louis, 1971

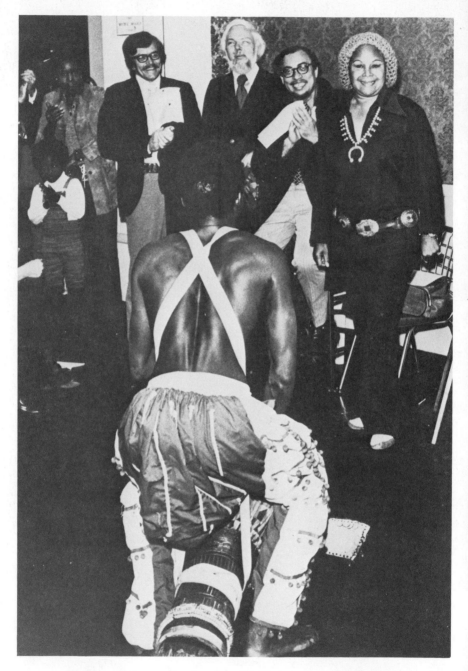

With participants in the Arts Conference, being officially welcomed by Mor Phiam, master percussionist from Senegal, 1971

Onstage with veteran musician Eubie Blake, during the finale of the world premiere of Scott Joplin's opera **Treemonisha**, *in Atlanta, Georgia, 1972*

Junior members of the Performing Arts Company on railroad tracks in East St. Louis, 1971

Facade of the Katherine Dunham Museum, before its opening in 1976

Returning to the United States meant making arrangements with the Internal Revenue Service to start paying some of the back income taxes she owed. Katherine made these arrangements because she felt she had to be able to go back to her native land. The book publishers were there. Most of the members of the former Dunham Dance Company were there. Hollywood was there. If she was going to make money, she had to be in the United States again. So Katherine Dunham ended her all-too-brief exile and resumed her active career.

While working in Hollywood, she continued writing the first volume of her autobiography, sending the chapters on to her agent in New York as she completed them. At last the good news came that the publisher Harcourt Brace was interested enough in her manuscript to offer her a contract, provided that she agreed to do a lot of rewriting. She agreed, got her contract, and almost immediately set off for Haiti and Habitation Leclerc. Only there, she decided, could she find the peace she needed to do the necessary rewriting on her book.

Reunited with her husband and daughter, living in the place she loved most on earth, Katherine Dunham was happy and productive. She worked rapidly on the rewriting of her book, and by the end of 1958 she had turned in the final draft of the volume she had decided to title *A Touch of Innocence*. The money she received from Harcourt Brace gave her a small financial cushion and soon she was deeply involved in a new project in Haiti—the opening of a free medical clinic.

Medical services for the poor in Haiti were practically nonexistent. Clinics were few and far between, understaffed, and not funded to dispense free medicines. All kinds of diseases were rampant, and infant mortality was high.

Katherine had been aware of these conditions ever since she had first visited Haiti, but it was not until early 1959 that it occurred to her to try to do something about them. She heard about a poor young couple whose baby had died because it had taken them so long to find and buy the medicine needed and to find a doctor to administer that medicine. She wrote to her doctor in New York about the medical situation for the poor in Haiti, and was surprised and delighted when he sent a huge supply of medicine samples. Immediately, she turned part of Habitation Leclerc into a free clinic, and with the help of two local doctors threw herself into caring for the ailing poor, working as hard at this activity as she had at her dancing and her writing.

But before long her money problems forced her to return to the stage. She re-formed the Dunham Dance Company, got a booking agent to line up a tour, and in 1959 she and her company began their third trip to Europe. It was a greater disaster than the Australia-Orient tour, with money problems and personality conflicts causing the group to split up in Vienna, Austria, before the tour was over. Fortunately for Katherine, her book was published at the end of 1959, and she could take comfort in the good reviews it received, although it never became the bestseller she had hoped it would be.

Katherine returned to Haiti and concentrated on making Habitation Leclerc a tourist attraction. She supervised the construction of some bungalows where guests could stay, a bar, a nightclub restaurant, and even a small zoo. By 1961 the resort was ready for business, but it could not have opened at a worse time. Haiti's government had changed hands again. Its new ruler, François Duvalier, known as Papa Doc, was a dictator who ran the country with an iron hand. His private militia terrorized the rich and poor both, and he and his followers used the foreign aid that came from other countries not to help their nation but to benefit themselves. Although Duvalier respected Katherine and did not make any trouble for her directly, indirectly he ruined her chances for making Habitation Leclerc a going tourist concern. Tourists did not like Haiti under Duvalier. There were too many beggars and a sense of fear and despair in the country that was not what people on vacation wanted to feel.

Once again, Katherine had to find another way to make money. She sent an outline for the second volume of her autobiography to Harcourt Brace, but the publisher wanted something more solid before issuing a contract or an advance. She didn't have the financial resources to work on the book without an advance. She had to return to the stage.

Stephen Papich had once been a student at the Dunham school in New York. Now he was a successful Hollywood producer, but he had kept in touch with Katherine, as nearly all her students and troupe members had. He suggested that she do another big revue that would open on Broadway and then tour in other parts of the United States. After all, it had been six years since her last Broadway appearance. Katherine was skeptical at first. It would be a lot of work, and she wondered if the time was right, in the early 1960s, for the type of big revue that had been so popular in the 1940s and 1950s. But the more she thought about it, the more she warmed to the idea. How about an African theme? she suggested to Papich. Soon, she had decided to feature some wonderful dancers she had seen in Morocco and was trying to figure out how to get the King of Morocco, Hassan II, to give his consent. And by the spring of 1962 she had John Pratt, Stephen Papich and several others traveling throughout western Africa lining up 25 dancers, musicians and singers to bring their talents to the show. Meanwhile, the Dunham old-timers were contacted, and quite a number of them returned to the fold. John Pratt would be doing the sets and costumes. The show would be a blend of old and new, and Katherine was excited about its possibilities. "It's my best work," she said, "and I'm not only excited about it but what it can lead to eventually."

The revue, *Bamboche,* opened at the 54th Street Theatre in New York on October 22, 1962, and it was as close to being a complete statement of her ideas about anthropology and dance as Katherine had ever achieved. It was a statement that she felt needed very much to be made, because she did not like the trends she was seeing in American dance. "I'm distressed at what has happened to dancers here since I began my work," she told a reporter for the New York *Herald Tribune.* "Oh, yes, they are better technicians. Physically, they can do anything you ask them. But something is missing. Spirit? Dedication? You name it." With the help of native African dancers and with American dancers trained in the Dunham technique, Katherine hoped to show America what was missing in its dance.

The show was divided into three parts. In the first act, Katherine introduced to America the dancers of Morocco, who were not a company like the Dunham Dance Company, nor a court company for King Hassan II of Morocco, but simply the best dancers from many villages and regions who were called upon to perform before the king on special occasions and who the king had said could dance in Katherine's show. They presented a combination of Moroccan tribal and regional dances. Katherine had suggested to King Hassan that this might be the beginning of a national dance theater in Morocco.

The second act was a dance-drama combining dances

from Central and South Africa with a political story about the movement for independence that was sweeping Africa at the time.

The third act featured American music and dancing and contained many old favorites from past Dunham revues, including "The Cakewalk" and "Barrelhouse Blues."

All in all, it was, as one critic put it, "gorgeously staged . . . a slick combination of blatant showmanship and honest-to-goodness folklore." Another critic wrote that: "The youngsters will learn from the lady herself what she means about 'spirit' in the Dunham way of dance, in this particular case a lowdown bezazz that technique alone cannot muster." There was praise, too, for Katherine Dunham herself. She was 51 years old now, still plagued by arthritis and by knee problems which several operations had been unable to cure completely, troubled too with a weight problem, but looking as lithe and subtle and sexy in her abbreviated costumes as a woman decades younger.

But the audiences did not flock to *Bamboche* as they had to the Dunham shows of earlier years, and then a newspaper strike killed all hopes of attracting an audience with lots of print publicity. With all seven major New York newspapers shut down from December 1962 to the middle of March 1963, producer Stephen Papich had no way to attract an audience. Mounting bills for salaries and theater rental could not be offset by ticket revenues. Papich was forced to close the show.

Again out of work and in need of money, Katherine did not despair. She was determined to keep her dancing technique and its spirit alive, and if the newspapers had prevented her from accomplishing her aim by means of a big revue, then she would find some other way to do it. She decided to revive the Dunham dance school.

She rented extra space in the Chelsea Hotel, where she

was staying, and advertised that she was in business again. Soon, she had attracted a group of students. But the other residents of the hotel, which had a reputation for allowing just about anything to go on so long as it was done for the sake of art, protested violently against the sound of bongo drums at all hours of the day. Katherine had to find another place for her school, and soon she had rented a studio at 440 West 42nd Street, where her percussionists could play the bongos anytime they liked. Then she was asked to choreograph the dances for the Metropolitan Opera's production of *Aïda,* and things seemed to be looking up for Katherine indeed.

She chuckles when she remembers her first meeting with Rudolf Bing, director of the Metropolitan Opera: "He said, 'Have you done any opera before?' and I sat there raking my mind to think if I'd done *anything* at all. Finally, I said no, and he said, 'Good. Because I want someone who has not done anything in opera before.' "

Katherine approached choreographing an opera just as she did her ethnic dancing:

I went back as far as I could in history and studied drawings and reports of ethnological and archeological findings, and I used these for movements and designs.

And then for the army's triumphal march, I thought surely that crossing such a large part of Africa, this army would have picked up people from different tribal groups along the way. So I put these different tribal groups in the returning army, which made it very exciting.

In her travels, Katherine had been to Morocco, where she had seen that country's "blue women," who dye their skin and their costumes with indigo. She had been impressed when she saw them, and she decided to put them into the triumphal march in *Aïda*. They would open the march with an offering of golden wheat sheaves. "It was really stunning," she recalls.

Unfortunately, hardly any of the critics liked her dances for the opera. Even critics who usually liked what she did criticized her for putting too much "voodoo" into them and trying to distract the audience from the music of the opera. But as one critic pointed out:

No one is ever really satisfied with the dances in any production of *Aïda*. . . . Taken together, ancient Egypt, 19th-century Italian music and the conventions of operatic spectacle are simply incompatible with any style of dancing known to man. They always have been and always will be.

Blame the Metropolitan, therefore, if you don't like the Dunham dances, but don't blame her. She has not changed her stripes, she has not stinted on her efforts and she has not shortchanged the management.

Apparently, the people at Southern Illinois University felt the same way as this critic did, for a year and a half later they asked Katherine to choreograph and stage a second opera, *Faust*, at their campus in Carbondale. Katherine agreed to do it, not knowing that her stay in Illinois would open the curtain on a whole new stage in her life.

She and John made preparations to stay in Illinois for several months, and Katherine regretfully closed her school. She had every intention of reopening it later, though, because it had become very important to her to keep the Dunham technique alive by teaching it to succeeding generations of young dancers.

TWELVE

ARRIVING AT THE SIU CAMPUS IN CARBONDALE IN 1964, KATHER-ine felt in many ways as if she was coming home. Carbondale was much farther south than Chicago and Joliet, but what were a few hundred miles to a woman who had traveled the world? Over the years, she had come to think of the whole state as her original home—largely because people in Japan or Latin America, Haiti or Trinidad, were not likely to have heard of Joliet, or even Chicago. It was a lot easier just to say, "Illinois, one of the United States."

She was given a wonderful welcome at the university, which opened all its facilities to her, and it wasn't long before she had decided to make a gift of her memorabilia to SIU. University officials were excited and pleased, at first, but as the Dunham memorabilia began to arrive, they started to get worried. How were they going to find room?

Katherine recalls, "As our baggage began to come in—all those tons and tons of artifacts and memorabilia and costumes from touring—Carbondale decided they couldn't take all these things plus the writings and special books and archives."

She didn't want her artifacts and papers split up. She wanted them to be housed together somewhere. So, she began looking for a place that had room for them all. "At the suggestion of Delyte Morris, who was then president of the whole Southern Illinois University complex, I went to the SIU branch at Edwardsville to see about making a base for us."

Once Katherine was in Edwardsville, it was not long before she visited East St. Louis, Illinois, a few miles to the south. R. Sargent Shriver, head of the federal government's Office of Economic Opportunity, suggested that she go there and see if she thought some sort of cultural arts program could be started in this city, where no such programs existed.

Katherine Dunham had seen a lot of depressing sights in her travels around the world. She had seen poverty and despair and decay. But East St. Louis was a revelation even to her, of how degraded people can become when they feel nobody cares about them.

East St. Louis has a long history as a sort of stepchild to St. Louis, Missouri, across the Mississippi River. It was originally a ferry station. In the late 1800s, with the arrival of the railroad and the Eads Bridge, which connected it to St. Louis, it became a transportation and meat-packing center. Although it was strong economically, even then it was considered more a place to work than a place to live.

Blacks began to arrive in East St. Louis in large numbers around 1917, after the United States entered World War I. The steel, glass and building materials factories of the city were booming with work under government contracts. Blacks from the South settled near the railroad yards and got factory jobs. Whites, angry at seeing these factories employ black workers, turned on the blacks. In July 1917, in one of the worst race riots in American history up to that time, mobs of whites attacked the blacks of East St. Louis, stabbing, clubbing and hanging them, and driving 6,000 from their homes.

But the East St. Louis riot of 1917 did not stop blacks from moving into the city, and by the time Katherine Dunham and John Pratt arrived in 1964, East St. Louis was well over 60 percent black. The city also had all the problems that go along with that kind of population statistic— the flight of whites to the suburbs, high unemployment, falling tax revenues, high crime rates, block upon block of burned-out or boarded-up buildings. East St. Louis looked like a city that was going out of business.

Its residents, especially the younger ones, were angry, and they had support for their anger among other black people across the country. It was the time of the major civil-rights movement. In the South, blacks were marching to demand equal treatment and conducting voting drives to assure their constitutional rights. The movement started as a nonviolent one, but by 1964 whites were meeting nonviolence with violence, killing and beating civil-rights workers. In the North, blacks in the cities had begun to demand their rights in a more violent way. In the summer of 1964 there were black riots in many American cities, and other cities, like East St. Louis, were like powder kegs awaiting just one spark to touch them off.

Katherine Dunham looked at conditions in East St. Louis and felt depressed. What depressed her even more was the way the community reacted to these conditions. "I was shocked at the violence, the rage so often turned inward on the community itself. It was so disheartening, all those young men going up in flames." But she did not feel helpless in the face of seemingly insurmountable problems.

Instead, she began thinking about how to improve conditions there. The logical place to start, she felt, was with the young people. They were putting all their thought and energy into crime and street-gang activity and destructive things. Some way had to be found to channel their energy into constructive activities, and naturally it was her idea that this way could be found through dance.

In the face of the urban riots in the North and the white violence against civil-rights workers in the South, President Lyndon Johnson and the U.S. Congress were enacting many laws to provide money for programs to make living conditions better for minorities. Katherine Dunham knew very well how one young black girl had benefited from the help of foundation grants and scholarships, and she had every hope that money from the government and other funding sources would indeed make a difference in the lives of minority people.

She went back to Carbondale and, while continuing her work choreographing and rehearsing the opera *Faust*, drew up a proposal for a Performing Arts Training Center in East St. Louis. She explained in the proposal that "East St. Louis has been the focal point of racial resentments, riots, delinquency and poverty for many years. Its situation close to the metropolis of St. Louis and still deprived of the benefits usually emanating from a metropolis because of its high Negro population, has kept the area a sensitive one."

There was a need, she continued, to replace crime and delinquency with more healthy objectives—discipline of body and mind, determination to work for a goal, ability to rise out of poverty and despair. She then went on to propose a school in East St. Louis that would be much like the other schools she had operated—a school that would teach anthropology, languages, percussion and dance. But unlike her other schools, learning to dance would not be the main objective: "The project presented here reaches far beyond dance in the popular definition. . . . Dance as it would serve the East St. Louis project is concerned with the fundamentals of human society."

The opera *Faust* was presented by the student dancers at SIU, Carbondale, in February 1965. Katherine had chosen very stark staging for this age-old story about a man who sells his soul to the devil in exchange for pleasures on earth. Reading over the story, she had been reminded of Adolf Hitler. He had done such terrible things to people that it had always seemed to her that he expected to go to Hell after he died, and so had nothing to lose.

There wasn't much opportunity to bring ethnic dancing to this production. But there was a good chance to bring to it interpretative dancing, and that is what Katherine chose to do. She had the dancers interpret bodies in a concentration camp, for example—they hung from wires, were draped over the stumps of trees, lay on the ground, all in absolutely frozen positions. There were scenes in which the dancers played carousing Nazis and their women, partying crazily while millions died. In the end, the devil, portrayed by a motorcyclist in a black leather jacket, roars across the stage to claim the soul of Dr. Faustus.

It was an exciting show, and if the student performers were too amateurish to fulfill Katherine's vision of the opera, her staging and choreography also helped to elevate the evening beyond a mere student production.

Once *Faust* was produced, Katherine Dunham's ties with Southern Illinois University did not end. She wanted to be close to her memorabilia, wherever they were housed, and the university wanted to maintain its association with this famous and respected dancer/choreographer/anthropologist. The university offered Katherine the position of Visiting Artist in the Fine Arts Division of Southern Illinois University at Edwardsville. Using this title, and with the backing of SIU, she submitted her proposal for a Performing Arts Training Center in East St. Louis. She began sending out her proposal to various funding sources, including the federal government, in March 1965, about a month after the production of *Faust*. She also gave a lecture at SIU in which she urged that a department of dance be established and given the university's full support.

The university had agreed to allow Katherine full freedom to continue her outside work, and knowing that it would be some time before there was any action on her East St. Louis project proposal, she accepted a variety of invitations to dance or teach or choreograph over the next two years.

One invitation was to choreograph the movie *The Bible*, which was to be filmed in Rome. As was her custom, Katherine managed to get several members of her former company into the film. This movie was the last, as of this writing, that she choreographed. "I was very happy with it," she says. "Eventually, I think, all dance on film will have to be done by dancers."

She choreographed a stage show in Rome for actor Marcello Mastroianni, who gave her a fragment of sculpture as a thank-you. She shipped it to Habitation Leclerc as the centerpiece for her private garden. She then choreographed a stage show in Paris and later gathered her entire company together again to perform in New York on the 25th anniversary of the American Ballet Theatre.

Her toughest and also her most rewarding assignment between 1965 and 1967 required her to go to Africa. The

First World Festival of Negro Arts was going to be held in Dakar, Senegal, in northwestern Africa, in 1965 and 1966. Katherine was sent by the U.S. State Department, at the request of the president of Senegal, to help train the Senegalese National Ballet and to act as general adviser to the president concerning the festival.

Katherine eagerly accepted the invitation. The job would be a challenge, and she looked forward to spending time in an African country that was similar to Haiti in its history of French colonialism and in its resultant mixture of African and French culture. She and John rented a home in a beautiful residential section of Dakar and went about collecting Senegalese artifacts to furnish it.

The main difficulty with her job in Senegal was the politics surrounding the festival. President Senghor of Senegal and others wanted to present pure expressions of the arts of their cultures, and to develop a separate black culture based on their own traditions. But Katherine's experiences had shown that such pure expressions were scarce in the modern world. She had seen Haitian dancers perform African dances with greater accuracy than African dancers did. Katherine managed to remain firm in her commitment to a more universal concept of culture without angering any important people, and in doing so she was carrying on a tradition of her own.

Katherine Dunham has managed somehow to remain true to her own ideals even in the face of intense pressure, and to make very few political enemies in the process. She managed to blend anthropology and dance in spite of the objections of anthropologists and dancers, and won the majority of both groups to her point of view. She managed on her own to desegregate theaters and hotels in the United States, at least for her company. Probably her greatest such achievement up to that time was managing to navigate the political squalls in Haiti. Few others, whether Haitians or non-Haitians, had been able to keep the respect and goodwill of the successive governments of that restless and strife-torn country. Katherine managed even to be on the good side of François Duvalier, the most tyrannical leader the island had known in many years, and she was not afraid to upset that delicate relationship when she had something to say.

While choreographing in Illinois, Paris, Rome, New York, and Dakar, she was also at work on a book about Haiti. She had a contract for it and she intended to say just what she thought about Duvalier and his predecessors, Estimé and Magloire. She did, however, stay pretty much away from Haiti while writing the book, feeling that she needed the geographical distance if she were to be objective in her writing. While in Dakar, she found she missed Habitation Leclerc, and felt almost disloyal to it. She united the two in a symbolic way. She planted herbs from Habitation Leclerc in her garden in Dakar, and she sprinkled soil from her yard in Dakar over the soil of Habitation Leclerc.

THIRTEEN

KATHERINE DUNHAM AND JOHN PRATT SPENT NEARLY A YEAR in Senegal. Katherine grew to love the country so much that once she finished her book she would happily have divided her time between Senegal and Haiti. But in 1967 news from the United States brought a pull that she could not resist: funding had come through for the proposed Performing Arts Training Center in East St. Louis. She could start another school, be close to her memorabilia, and maybe finish her book at last. Soon, Katherine and John had packed up and were on their way to East St. Louis. With them was Jeanelle Stovall, who was a simultaneous translator at the United Nations when she met Katherine during a vacation in Senegal in 1965. They had liked each other so much that when her vacation was over, Jeanelle had not returned to her job. Instead, she had taken a leave of absence in order to work with Katherine in Dakar. Now, she wanted to work with Katherine in East St. Louis.

Funding for the center was to come from three sources. The university, whose officials had been moved by Katherine's lecture about the importance of a dance department, and which felt a responsibility to do something to help improve conditions for young people in East St. Louis, would provide the basic support. Other grants would be given by the Rockefeller Foundation and the Danforth Foundation of St. Louis for a period of two years.

What this funding provided for was a house where Katherine and John could live and set up offices as well as another project, the Dynamic Museum, where costumes, artifacts and other memorabilia collected in their travels could be displayed. The house was located in Alton, several miles north and west of East St. Louis. Katherine remembered Alton from her childhood. When she was 12, she and her stepmother had taken a wonderful road trip in the Dunhams' new car to visit relatives of Annette's there. The relatives were long since dead, but there was still a special place in Katherine's heart for Alton, Illinois.

The Dynamic Museum was a project that was especially close to the hearts of Katherine Dunham and John Pratt. It represented so much of the years they had spent together: artifacts, costumes, posters, programs, records and films that recorded the history of their work and that of the Dunham dancers. They wanted to share this material with other people. They wanted people to be able to touch it and interact with it in a personal or dynamic way. That is why they decided to call it the Dynamic Museum. John Pratt was the official curator.

University and foundation funding also provided for a pilot project under which 50 high school students were chosen to receive instruction at the infant Performing Arts Training Center, and five counselors were chosen to be trained by Katherine Dunham to, in turn, train the students. This pilot project had very little to do with dance, but Katherine realized at the outset that if she came into the community proclaiming some sort of dance renaissance, she would be laughed across the Eads Bridge, if not into the murky waters of the Mississippi.

Arriving back in East St. Louis after several years in Rome, Paris, New York and Dakar, Katherine found that things had not changed much there. If anything, conditions were worse.

> East St. Louis was in a serious state of decay at that time, and I found that discouraging in a way, because like so many people my age, I thought the civil rights movement was going to change everything. And then, I'd been in Africa for a year . . . and to return to find that the situation was worse than it had ever been, that the violence was so heightened, was shocking.

Katherine Dunham returned to find the young people she wanted to reach even more alienated than they had been two years earlier. "Their violence and rage was so often turned inward on the community itself," she recalls, and the results seemed all negative—more burned-out and boarded-up buildings, more fights and killings, more idle young people standing on the corners of streets.

No wonder the university decided to house Katherine and John in Alton. Who in his right mind would put two famous world travelers in their fifties in the middle of East St. Louis?

Katherine was aware that she could not just go out into the streets of East St. Louis and get the young people to follow her like some motherly Pied Piper. So she chose not to have a lot of direct contact with the 50 high school students in the beginning. She would reach them through grown-up counselors, people especially chosen for their ability to bridge the gap between herself and the kids.

These counselors had to be mature enough to know that the world was much larger than East St. Louis, and that if you didn't realize that you needed discipline to cope with this larger world, you were in real trouble. To be able to transmit their knowledge to the kids of East St. Louis these counselors had to have some similar experiences to theirs. In looking for counselors, Katherine was seeking not college degrees but degrees from the proverbial "school of hard knocks." Two of the five she chose were former prison inmates.

These ex-convicts did not suddenly start doing pirouettes, either. Dance training was a far-off step in the Dunham pilot program. The first step was to get the 50 students interested enough to come back, on their own, to a program that they knew was meant to help them learn something. If that meant teaching them karate and African drumming, rather than classical ballet and the history of music, then that's what they would be taught. As Katherine explains, "We were trying to get the young people involved in things that would direct their energies in alternative ways, in ways that would be good for the community and not so self-destructive."

To her mind, there was rhythm and discipline in karate and judo, and so these were not inappropriate courses to be taught in the new Performing Arts Training Center. They certainly were popular. "The young men went in strongly for karate and judo," she recalls. She began to call them her "magnets," ways to attract the youngsters, first to the center itself and eventually to the dance.

Katherine also found that she carried a certain aura because she had just come from Africa. These young people who ordinarily had very little use for old people and who couldn't care less about Katherine's fame as a dancer-choreographer, were very admiring of her African experience.

The times were very difficult in terms of race relations. The young person was far more interested in the situation of black versus white than in the arts. We were seen not so much as artists as people with recent, close ties to Africa. All the young people we came into contact with at that time had a strong wish to become affiliated with Africa. So we offered courses in African drums, and we displayed African sculpture and African-originated dances. It gave them a feeling of identification. So that made it easier for us to work with them. The young man who might be out on a bombing raid one night would probably be in on a drumming class the next.

But it was a slow process. There was an excitement about that era of destructive militancy that attracted the energies of the city's youth. Burning and destroying seemed much more obvious ways to act out their anger than dancing and drumming. Katherine recalls, "For three years we had a really rough time getting the young people to become interested in the cultural arts. Those long, hot summers!"

FOURTEEN

IT WAS HARD FOR KATHERINE DUNHAM TO SIT BACK AND NOT take a more personal, direct role in trying to reach the young people of East St. Louis. It was not enough just to be someone who was admired because she had spent a year in Africa. Before long, she had plunged right into the thick of things in East St. Louis.

She and John Pratt moved from the house in Alton to a home in East St. Louis. "It was too hard for me being so far away from the community where I wanted to work," says Katherine. They moved into the heart of the city's ghetto, to a house whose ground-floor windows were boarded up and whose chief view was vacant lots and boarded-up buildings. But at least it was close to the people Katherine wanted to reach. Then she went about finding ways to attract more of the youth of the community to her program.

One of the original 50 students chosen for the pilot project was Darryl Braddix, a bright young man who was a member of a street gang called the Imperial War Lords. Katherine hoped to reach other members of the gang through him, and during a time when her daughter, Marie

Christine, was visiting she arranged that she, her daughter, and Jeanelle Stovall would meet Darryl and some other members of the gang one night in July at a nearby tavern. That was the night Katherine was arrested.

The meeting went just fine. The women listened to what the gang members had to say about what they thought would motivate them and the other youth of the city. Then they offered ideas about what the Performing Arts Training Center could do to meet the needs of the young people. Armed with ideas and hope, the two sides adjourned the meeting, and Darryl Braddix offered to walk the women back to their car. There, the police confronted him and arrested him on the spot.

"What are the charges?" Katherine Dunham wanted to know. The arresting officers told her to mind her own business. She would not hear of it. She told Marie Christine to take the car and go home. She and Jeanelle would accompany Darryl to the police station.

At the station, Katherine wanted to know if Darryl was going to have the right to call a lawyer. When the officer at the booking desk ignored her, she stepped behind the desk and demanded an answer. The dispatcher told her she had no business behind the desk. Katherine said she had no intention of moving until she knew what the charges against Darryl were and when he was going to be able to call a lawyer.

During all this time, no one told the police that this troublesome woman was Katherine Dunham. The officers might not have been familiar with her name, but they might have backed off a bit if they'd been told that she was internationally famous. No one told them who she was. Katherine and Jeanelle believed they were acting as ordinary citizens and shouldn't have to pull rank. Darryl Braddix, for all his willingness to work with Katherine, was probably hoping the experience would be an education for her and help her to understand better what it was like to be a youth in East St. Louis. Whatever the reasons, Katherine Dunham was treated badly by the officers. She later told newspaper reporters, "One cop started pushing me around and two other big cops started twisting my arms. I asked if I were under arrest and they said, 'You sure are!' "

Fifty-eight-year-old Katherine Dunham, internationally renowned as a prime mover behind ethnic dance, was booked on charges of disorderly conduct. Then an officer picked her up bodily and carried her to a second-floor cell, where she spent three and a half hours before Marie Christine and John Pratt managed to get her released on bond.

The incident made national headlines: "Katherine Dunham is Jailed 3 ½ Hours Following Protest" read the headline in the New York *Times*. East St. Louis officials were highly embarrassed. They quickly dropped all charges against those involved, but the incident had left a bad taste in the mouths of just about everyone. To make amends, the leaders of East St. Louis decided to present Katherine with the official key to the city.

Katherine accepted it, knowing full well that it was the only way the authorities could think of to say they were sorry. If taking it had meant just relieving them of their guilt, she would have thought twice about giving them, and their police department, such an easy way out. But Katherine saw the whole incident and the publicity surrounding it as another kind of key—one that might help open that invisible door between her program and the people she wanted to reach. And sure enough, the Imperial War Lords and other gangs, and the poor black community as a whole, began to believe in her then. She had stood up for one of them, and thus what she had to say was worth a hearing.

The fledgling Performing Arts Training Center began to take shape after that. The East St. Louis community did not flock to it, but people began to trickle in. While the young men were still only interested in the martial arts, the young women were more receptive to dance. They brought along their younger brothers and sisters, usually because there was no one else to look after them, and Katherine started classes for young children to meet this new need.

Progress was slow. There were problems attracting students, attracting teachers, just setting up the structure of the center. But Katherine Dunham had some advantages in taking on her tremendous task. There was her own fame—and she did not mind using it in a good cause. Some students, and parents of potential students, came to the center because she was there. And there were all the dancers and musicians who had been part of the Dunham Dance Company at one time or another. In spite of the difficulties the company had been through over the years, almost all the former members of the company felt a strong loyalty to "Miss Dunham." Soon, they began to arrive in East St. Louis to help out.

One of the first to come was one of the most famous members of the Dunham Dance Company—Lenwood Morris. The soft-spoken former lead dancer would remain associated with the Performing Arts Training Center almost continually until his early and tragic death in March 1981. Others would come for a semester or two, lending their special skills and talents to the young enterprise and attracting more students with their offerings of special courses in percussion and movement and ethnic culture.

With the arrival of these reinforcements, Katherine decided she could take a little time off to finish her book on Haiti. She'd thought she could come to East St. Louis and finish it in three months, but with all her responsibilities it took a good year. The book, *Island Possessed*, was published by Doubleday & Company in 1969. Dedicated to John Pratt and to the Republic of Haiti, it was, as Katherine wrote, "written with love" and explained, she thought, "many things about this author and about that island."

Although it never became a bestseller, the book received fine critical reviews, including one from President François Duvalier, who wrote to Katherine to thank her for loving his country. Katherine was relieved at his reaction, though she would not have changed a word of the book with the president's response in mind. With the book published, she felt free to return to Haiti and Habitation Leclerc. Regretfully, she and John gave up their house in Dakar, which they had continued to lease after going to East St. Louis. They had to choose the two places that meant most to them, and they chose Haiti because they loved it and East St. Louis because it needed them.

As time went on, the people of East St. Louis responded to the obvious sincerity of Katherine Dunham's desire to help. Her arrest scored big points. This was obviously a tough lady who was ready to go to bat for the people of the community. According to Valerie Gettis, who first arrived at the center in the early years: "Just about anything would have been great for us, because before she came there was nothing here for poor people." Others heard about Katherine, decided to "check her out," and stayed.

Girls like Valerie came to dance. But it was a long time before the boys would dance. Katherine recalls:

> They loved to come and drum, and then they began asking what other courses were being taught. Sometimes they would get interested in painting. And some

strange things would happen—like the time a whole group of them asked if they could take a course in the Japanese language from our karate teacher. They had become so interested in karate that they wanted to learn the proper Japanese terminology. So, for a whole summer, Japanese was taught. We've always had African instructors, so we've been able to offer the Yoruba language and Senegalese.

In the early days, Katherine even used drama as one of her "magnets" to get kids off the streets.

I can say for sure that we were responsible for breaking up a drug district called "The Corner." We used to recruit down there. We were rehearsing on a nearby high school stage. They got interested in drama. They made up their own scenes. They did cantata-form musicals about their own folk heroes, the people from their own streets.

Recognition of the work of the center from outside East St. Louis helped to gain it the acceptance of the East St. Louis community. In 1968 the University of Chicago Alumni Association presented Katherine with its Professional Achievement Award, and Katherine took the opportunity to talk about her latest work. The people of East St. Louis appreciated that. But what really caused them to sit up and take notice was the occasion of the 1970 White House Conference on Children, and the fact that Katherine took the opportunity to showcase the children of the community.

Katherine recalls when she was approached by the organizers of the conference. "They asked me if I would choreograph something or present something black. I said I would gladly do it if I could use East St. Louis children, and they said that was fine. So we had auditions at the center."

It took quite a bit of community cooperation just to hold auditions and rehearsals for all the children. Their parents were often unable to escort them, because they either worked or had to stay home with other children or could not afford the transportation costs. The Performing Arts Training Center had no buses.

"So, police cars provided the transportation," Katherine recalls. "But there were problems with that at first. Children would be waiting at the school for transportation to the center and a police car would drive up, and the kids would refuse to get in! We finally got things settled. The city really rose to that occasion, I must say."

Some 43 children and about a dozen mothers went to Washington with Katherine and her teachers. There were 67 in the group altogether, the children ranging from 4 to 13. They were chosen either because they were quite skilled at karate and percussion and African dance or else awfully cute in their attempts at these disciplines. "Of course we stole the show," Katherine remembers with a chuckle, "but it was a hair-raising experience in some ways. To get ready for an onstage rehearsal there in Washington, we had to round up all those wild little boys in the halls of the hotels. . . . Our performance was filmed, and I expect it is in the National Archives."

More children began to arrive at the center after that, some brought by their parents, others finding their own way. Older youth came, too, and more former members of the Dunham Dance Company arrived to teach for at least a semester. As the Performing Arts Training Center continued to grow and to demand more of her time, Katherine was forced to make the regretful decision to put aside for a while her dreams for her Dynamic Museum.

"The first year of its operation, the university funded it," she explains, "but it didn't really seem to fit into any of their various programs, so we were left to do it independently."

There wasn't room in the house in East St. Louis, there was no money for staff, and neither Katherine nor John felt they could take the time away from their work at the center to devote proper attention to the collection. They mounted small displays from time to time, but from 1971 to the end of 1977, the Dynamic Museum and its rich contents were unavailable to the general public. Faced with the choice between concentrating on things and concentrating on people, Katherine did what she'd done all her life: she chose people.

It was sometimes hard to coordinate all the responsibilities she had taken on. Not only was the center like her earlier schools in its wide range of course offerings—languages and percussion, anthropology and theatrical movement—it was both a branch of a large university and a sort of neighborhood settlement house. Any SIU student who was eligible could take courses there, usually with an aim toward becoming a dancer or a teacher of dance. At the same time, anyone from the East St. Louis community could take the courses. But Katherine always had executive ability. She managed to coordinate a well-structured program that succeeded in doing what it was supposed to do. Progress was slow, but it was definite. After two years, the Performing Arts Training Center had proved its worth.

During those first two years, the Rockefeller and Danforth foundations had provided "seed" money. Once the program was established, these foundation grants were not renewed. It was up to Southern Illinois University to support it, and the university did. In a time when major institutions like universities were making every effort to improve their image with poor and minority communities, the Performing Arts Training Center in East St. Louis was an important feather in SIU's cap. In Katherine's opinion, it still is: "I would say that the university's program in East St. Louis depends very heavily on the Performing Arts Training Center for its visibility."

The Performing Arts Training Center also proved to be something of which the people of East St. Louis came to be proud, for the center was the first arts institution in this city of 70,000. Today it and the Katherine Dunham Museum are the only two such cultural forces.

FIFTEEN

ON THE SURFACE, THINGS HAVEN'T CHANGED VERY MUCH IN East St. Louis. It still looks like a town that is going out of business. Unemployment is still high, the tax base is still eroding, crime is rampant. The city is still in such a poor financial situation that city workers do not always get paid on time and city services are poor, when they are rendered at all. There is still not a single movie theater in the community, and interaction between the people of East St. Louis and St. Louis right across the Eads Bridge is as minimal as ever—a situation that continues to amaze Katherine and John.

When they first arrived in East St. Louis, they did not understand how separate the two cities were. It took time for them to realize that the Mississippi might as well be the Pacific Ocean. Katherine recalls the time Butterfly McQueen was at the center. The black actress had played Scarlett O'Hara's maid in *Gone With the Wind*:

I thought some of the students might want to see *Gone With the Wind*. It was playing at one of the movie theaters in St. Louis, and I gave them money to go. About two weeks later they came and gave me some money. When I asked what it was for, they said it was the money for the movie. They hadn't gone, and when I asked why, they said, "We just don't go to St. Louis."

Katherine has learned to accept the fact that there are some attitudes she just cannot change. There are times when she gets very depressed.

I feel the drain of the constant negative influence that one can find when one looks for it. We can't change the economics of the city, and that of course is the main problem here. But we can help to give the people an outlook, to show them there is a larger world out there. We see positive development in single individuals and in some ways in whole groups of people.

Today, some 15 years after the Performing Arts Training Center began, East St. Louisians of all ages take advantage of its course offerings. By 1977, the number of community members enrolled in at least one course had reached almost 900, and now that number is well over 1,000.

There is a full-fledged dance company that performs at various SIU campuses as well as in neighboring cities like St. Louis. There is a junior troupe for six to thirteen year olds, who perform for local audiences. There are classes for children as young as four years old. They learn simple percussion, basic dance movements, and are encouraged to develop their imaginations. There are classes for senior citizens. "We have large groups of senior citizens who are learning to strengthen their bodies and limber their muscles through dance," says Katherine.

SIU students who want to become teachers of dance go out from the center to teach classes at local elementary and high schools. "We have a number of good teachers going out from the center," says Katherine, "and always requests for more."

A full-time professional staff of over 20 teachers instructs both community members and SIU students. It's an ever-changing staff, for Katherine encourages visiting instructors, especially people who have been part of her various dance companies. "There's always quite a turnover," she explains, "because a person who wants to be available for auditions in New York doesn't want to be away for too long. We've had people come for periods of time ranging from overnight to several years."

Lenwood Morris, who arrived a few weeks after the center began in 1967, was the instructor who stayed longest. He died in the early spring of 1981 and was mourned by everyone there and in the world of dance. Only a few months earlier he had won the Outstanding Ballet Master Award for 1980 in New York. Katherine, who'd known him since he joined her company in 1943, called him "Prince." A student at the center named Marlayne Simpson wrote, "To so many people his past, as dynamic as it was, did not matter, they only felt his warmth and knew how he affected *them*."

Another veteran teacher at the center is Mor Phiam, a master drummer and choreographer from Senegal. He has trained a number of students to be superb drummers. He has doubled, on occasion, as a teacher of Senegalese. He also choreographs some of the dances the Performing Arts Training Center company performs.

Others come and go. "I wish I could say that they come because of the program in East St. Louis," says Katherine. "I don't think I can, though. They still have that syndrome of the Dunham company and come chiefly because of me. Still, we've been operating since 1967. I hope they are committed in some way to the program, and prepared to carry on things themselves."

Some of the teachers who are most committed to the program have practically grown up in it. Katherine is especially proud of people like Doris Bennett. "She was just a child when she first came here. Now she's one of our lead teachers. She remained with us all the way through, until she now is a master teacher. I like to see them develop that way."

Another teacher at the center is Theodore Jamison. A former student there, he went to Haiti to perform and to learn more about dance, then spent time teaching in Mexico before returning to East St. Louis.

Other students trained at the center have gone on to careers as professional dancers. "We have one girl who went to Las Vegas," says Katherine. "Marsha Robinson got her master's degree in dance and theater here and now has made a career in nightclub work."

Others have gone on to Broadway and even the Muni Opera, and there is one young man whose success and versatility amaze even the successful and versatile Katherine Dunham.

Emilio La Estaria is from Peru. He came to us seven years ago, stayed five years, and got his master's degree in dance and theater at Edwardsville. He took all of his dance work here with us. Then he went to New York, enrolled in the pre-med course at Columbia, and is now in medical school. He still dances, and the amazing thing is that he still teaches. He somehow finds time to teach Dunham technique, and whenever we need him for a special performance he's available. PBS did a program a while back, called *The Divine Drumbeat—Katherine Dunham and Her People.* Emilio was the young man in the puberty dance.

One of the most promising students in the opinion of both Katherine and John was Darryl Braddix, the member of the Imperial War Lords who first showed an interest in the Performing Arts Training Center. It was his arrest by East St. Louis police that led to Katherine's night in jail back in 1967. Sadly, Darryl is no longer with the program. "He gave up," says Katherine. "I don't know why people get the idea that after you're 20 you're too old to dance. That's purely an American attitude. But I can't help feeling badly about people like Darryl. If they'd only started with us when they were younger, they might have felt more secure about staying on with us after they were older."

Katherine does keep in touch with Darryl Braddix and other young men who were gang members when she first met them. Many of these former gang members, who used to steal cars and smash windows because they had nothing better to do, have grown up to be young men who care about improving their community. "A number of them have gone pretty deeply into politics," says Katherine. "Part of their war during the 60s was against the corrupt political situation. Some of them are now in the political structure of the city."

There are still gangs in East St. Louis, of course. They are a powerful force, far more powerful than the "magnets" with which Katherine Dunham tries to lure members away from them. But every now and then, she manages to attract some youths away from the gangs. Their stories are almost always the same: after a few years most of their friends are either dead or in jail, and they are grateful to the center for demanding so much discipline and concentration that they didn't have either the time or the energy for gang activity.

There are many other former students who have not gone on in dance but who have benefited in other ways from the training they have received at the Performing Arts Training Center. Valerie Gettis went on to major in communications at SIU. Eugene Redmond gained the confidence he needed to pursue his interest in writing. He later toured the West Coast giving lectures and readings of his own poetry. What nearly all the students have gained from the Dunham program is a basic energy, a basic pride. She has always demanded much of herself, and she demands much from her students. They respond to her incredible vitality, and often find an energy in themselves that they never thought they had. As Dr. Glory Van Scott, another former student who teaches dance in New York, puts it, "I think if you really take her message, you will turn around and take the ball and go with it. You realize you are a worthwhile person, that your perimeter is not just where you live, that you can find a wider range."

Such statements make sense to Katherine Dunham. Dunham technique, she likes to point out, is not just a way to dance, it is a way of life.

Although her first allegiance was to the Performing Arts Training Center, Katherine did not give up her dream of a permanent museum for her artifacts and memorabilia. All during the mid-1970s, she worked to find outside funding sources. At last, a group of wealthy and influential supporters formed a group called "The Friends" to work on the project. They were able to acquire a Victorian mansion on Pennsylvania Avenue in East St. Louis to serve as a permanent home for her collection.

The museum opened in December 1977. The board of directors had voted to call it the Katherine Dunham Museum, but Katherine still calls it the Dynamic Museum "because we have conversation going on most of the time when groups are going through, and because most of the objects can be touched." Although there isn't sufficient staff for it to be open every day, on the days when it is open large number of school classes, senior citizens groups, and individual people visit. Katherine makes her presence felt there as often as her schedule permits.

A museum is one of the concrete expressions of a city's interest in art. I think it's terribly important for both the young and the old people of East St. Louis to be able to come out of their poverty environment and identify with their heritage and see what black cultures in other parts of the world have achieved.

Hopefully, the careful selection of the pieces and their tasteful arrangement will make the people of East St. Louis feel less isolated and will, perhaps more than anything else we've been doing here, give them a real feeling of hope. Beauty rubs off, you know.

# SIXTEEN

ONE OF THE THINGS THAT PLEASES KATHERINE DUNHAM MOST about the Performing Arts Training Center is that, unlike her earlier schools, it functions quite well without her. She is aware that some of the teachers and students come mainly because of her, but when she is out of the country or busy with other projects it operates smoothly, overseen by Jeanelle Stovall, who took a leave of absence from her job with the United Nations to work with Katherine over 15 years ago and has been with her ever since. Katherine is trying to take less and less of an active role in the day-to-day workings of the center.

"What I hope for is to be free from the responsibility of the company, let others take the responsibility, so I can write," she says. "I'm very interested in doing more writing now."

She is at work on a second volume of her autobiography. The first, *A Touch of Innocence*, was about her first 18 years. Her books on Haiti and on the Maroons included quite a bit of autobiographical material about the days when she majored in anthropology and did field work. This volume covers the period 1937 to 1947, after she had returned from the West Indies and was developing her dance company and doing her first serious choreography. "I'm calling it *The Mine Field*," she confides, "because every time I thought about how I felt in these years I realized I was always up against some obstacle. It was a period when dance was just beginning to take hold, when such a thing as black dance was practically nonexistent, and it was not easy touring those first few years."

It is an odd experience for her to go back and relive those years. Things are so very different now. Dance as an art form is recognized and supported all across the country. American modern dance is admired around the world for its vitality. Ethnic dance and black dance are as popular as classical ballet. There are major black dance companies, such as the Alvin Ailey Dance Company and Arthur Mitchell's Dance Theatre of Harlem. Most important, Katherine Dunham, more than any other single person, is credited with bringing all this about. As New York *Post* critic Clive Barnes wrote in early 1979, "What can one say about Katherine Dunham? This woman—she is going to be 70 this coming June—revolutionized American dance."

In the fall of 1978, Katherine learned that she would be presented with the 1979 Albert Schweitzer Music Award. The award had been instituted in 1975 and was to be given every four years. On January 14, 1975, the one-hundredth anniversary of the birth of the great humanitarian doctor and lover of music, the first award had been given to violinist Isaac Stern. Four years later, the second award was presented to Katherine Dunham: "For a life dedicated to music and devoted to humanity."

The presentation took place at Carnegie Hall in New York on January 15, 1979, Martin Luther King Day. There has also been a benefit program of dances spanning

Katherine's entire career and performed by three generations of Dunham dancers. The program was produced and directed by former Dunham dancer Dr. Glory Van Scott, but Katherine herself was needed to choreograph, to help round up the widely scattered former members of the Dunham company, and to provide the newest generation of Dunham dancers. Katherine was quick to accept the invitation. She was excited at the prospect of seeing a retrospective of her work and especially at the opportunity to showcase the work of her students in East St. Louis.

She and others involved in producing the benefit show began a period of intensive work, and it was probably most intensive for Katherine. The program included "The Cuban Suite" (1938), "Rites de Passage" (1938), "Los Indios" (1941), "Flaming Youth" (1942), the famous "Shango," a cakewalk number, and a dance to the music of Scott Joplin's tune "The Entertainer." Although there were former Dunham dancers who remembered the choreography of the early dances, it was up to Katherine, the original choreographer, to do most of the remembering. And she did not have extensive written records to aid her.

I don't write it down. I feel there's something impersonal about it. I do make notes. I film when I can, and I have my own system of drawings and stage positions. But mainly it is simply knowing thoroughly inside and out what the subject is, and then gradually the choreography impresses itself. But I had a hard time remembering all the choreography we had to use. I was astonished at how much choreography there is in our repertoire. It just seems endless.

The other hard part for Katherine was choosing the students from the center who would go to Carnegie Hall. She would have liked to have taken them all. She would have liked to have showcased the junior troupe and the senior citizens classes as well as the resident company. As it was, she could not even take the whole company. In the end several young women and seven young men who were at the East St. Louis center appeared at Carnegie Hall.

Katherine was proudest of the young men, for most of them had come from the streets and she had devoted much time and effort to winning them over. She finds that easier to do now: "Their attitude toward dance has probably changed because of companies like Alvin Ailey's. Also, we put them through such strenuous physical work that they don't think of dance anymore as being something just for girls." But it's still a struggle to win some young men with promise away from the street. One of the lead dancers Katherine took to New York from East St. Louis had started carrying a gun at the age of 12. He had almost been expelled from the center several times, and it had been touch and go whether he would go to Carnegie Hall at all. But Katherine had liked his temperament, his spirit. "You learn a lot on the street about people and about yourself," she explains. "Our students who are not from the street are slower, I think, at self-appreciation."

On the night of January 15, 1979, all the work and remembering and all the trust Katherine Dunham had put in her dancers over the years, came together and paid off. It was a wonderful evening for everyone involved. Eartha Kitt, who'd left the Dunham company in Paris many years earlier and gone on to stardom as a singer, narrated the program. Dunham stars from the 1930s like Vanoye Aikens and Lucille Ellis appeared onstage with East St. Louis youngsters, and with dancers from all the years in between, in classic numbers from the Dunham repertoire. The audience, which included other former Dunham stars and Dunham fans, gave two standing ovations to Katherine herself. She deserved and enjoyed every minute of both.

There have been other tributes to Katherine Dunham since then. There was a program about her on the Public Broadcasting System. Proceeds from the Carnegie Hall benefit went toward a matching grant from the National Endowment for the Arts to videotape Dunham dances. Some of her books, long out of print, are being reissued by new publishers. Meanwhile, the object of all this attention continues to live much as she has for the past 50 years— attending to her many interests with extraordinary energy.

Except for the Carnegie Hall gala, she has not done much choreography in the past few years. She did the choreography for the world premiere of Scott Joplin's opera *Treemonisha* in Atlanta in 1972, and up until three years ago she did a great deal of the choreographing for Southern Illinois University.

She does not do very much lecturing anymore either, because "I found that preparing a lecture, and getting to the place and getting back was just taking too much out of me." But when asked for her opinions about what is going on in the world, she is still very happy to give strong ones.

She is uncomfortable about the growing conservative trend that she sees developing not just in this country but throughout the world.

A conservative trend anywhere is hard on any new concept of politics, economics, morals, etc. All over the world, minority people are going to be under governments of extreme conservatism, and I think their fight for survival will be that much harder. One of the things conservatives do not feel is worth a great deal of money or attention is the development of what we know as Third World countries.

This conservative trend also causes her to worry about the future for young black people. Asked where she thinks they are headed, she replied:

I wish I knew. I was encouraged for a while by their great interest in other countries of the world. They had such high hopes for Africa and the independence movements there. But Africa didn't work out very well. There are so many problems—none of the newly independent countries have emerged as nations that black American youth can identify with.

I think their desire to be further educated is great, but they seem to think it will save the day for them, and I don't see that it will. After all this education, what on earth are they going to do with it? It's great to have it because you need it to compete, and for your own self-development. But I think somewhere along the line the politicians and adult black people had better find a way for young people to get jobs after they get this education. I find more and more that once black people reach a certain level of success, they don't want to look back. They don't want to help those they left behind.

The same could never be said about Katherine Dunham. All her life she has worked with and cared about people. She is just as interested in them as ever, but now that she is in her 70s there are things she wants to do for herself, and things that she wants to take time to enjoy.

Now that the Performing Arts Training Center is on its

feet, Katherine would like to spend more time in Haiti at Habitation Leclerc, writing and working to recreate the society of poets and artists that flourished on the island 30 or 40 years ago before political troubles caused most of these creative people to leave. Every creative person she meets and likes is invited to visit, either as her personal guest or as a paying guest in one of the five suites furnished for that purpose, and she is pleased that a small international community is beginning to develop in nearby Port-au-Prince. François Duvalier's son and successor, Jean-Claude Duvalier, has proved to be as great a tyrant as his father, but he, too, respects Katherine and her friends.

The most welcome "guest" of all at Habitation Leclerc is Marie Christine, who visits her parents at least a couple of times a year in East St. Louis and Haiti. Marie Christine lives in Rome. "She teaches dance and Dunham technique," says Katherine, "but chiefly she is a guitarist and a singer. She's in love with the guitar and wants that to be her career." Katherine is pleased that her daughter is a guitarist, because she is carrying on a family tradition. "My father played the guitar," Katherine explains, "and every time we've had an American section in a show there has been a guitar number."

Tradition is very important to Katherine, and the most important tradition to her is that of Haitian *vodun* or voodoo. She began studying it in her college days, when she first went to Haiti on a Rosenwald Fellowship. During that first visit she was initiated into the *vodun* cult, but it was just the first of many steps to be taken. Many non-Haitians, including anthropologists and writers, have gone through that first step, but very few have continued to study the religion. Katherine has. In fact, she is now studying it more deeply than ever.

She has a thatched-roof temple on the grounds of Habitation Leclerc, and she studies to be a high priestess there. Five years ago, she went through a second "fire" baptism, which brought her into the third stage of initiation. There are five stages in all.

Just to get where I am now I had to go through many years of just *lavê tête*—washing your head to get rid of your old spirit so that the god can come in and you can have a new spirit. Every initiation is like being born again—you are reduced to being a child. You're completely stripped of your personality and everything that you had. And then you are put back together again. This is what I like about it.

Some of Katherine Dunham's interest in *vodun* stems from her natural curiosity about Haitian culture. She is just finding out after all these years that there is a whole secret language in the use of the sacred rattle and bell—a language developed by the slaves because they were afraid to use the spoken word for fear that their masters would find out what they were doing. How much more authentic her Haitian dances could have been if she'd only known about this 30 or 40 years ago!

But a big part of Katherine's interest in *vodun* is personal. She explains:

I have a feeling that if I go into it deeply and sincerely, I will meet myself coming around the other way. I'll know more about dance, more about what I haven't been able to express. I feel that if I can master it as the Haitian *vodun* have mastered it, I will find a beauty that is far beyond what I have experienced of beauty otherwise. I am finding this higher beauty, and it's what I want.

* * *

After 70-odd years of living, Katherine Dunham is still "stretching." She is stretching her mind and her imagination and her soul just as in her dancing years she stretched the muscles and sinews of her body. Because she is still "stretching," she remains a powerful model for the young people at the Performing Arts Training Center. As former student Valerie Gettis once put it, "There's a basic energy . . . a basic pride . . . that she brings out . . . and it allowed me to stretch out in directions that I may not have gone into." Or, as former company member Dr. Glory Van Scott once said, "You realize you can find a wider range. You look at her and see what she has done, and is still doing, and you realize that you can—and must—do it, too."

But perhaps Katherine Dunham puts it best. In one simple statement she sums up her philosophy of life, her philosophy of dance, her philosophy behind her work at the Performing Arts Training Center in East St. Louis. It is this: "I am a firm believer in what human beings can do."

INDEX